POSITIVELY TRAUMATIZED

Positively Traumatized Self-Discovery

Written by

Julie Kundert/Hunter

Published in 2019 by Julie Kundert/Hunter
Email: jjewels2010@gmail.com
Instagram: juliekunderthunter

The cover of this book is a candid image of Julie and her oldest daughter Paige. They are celebrating their love for one another 7 years after their escape from the terrifying violence.

Part of the proceeds will go to Strength United Family Justice Center to help support survivors of domestic and sexual abuse.

ISBN: 978-0-578-21910-3

Editor: Libero Antonio Di Zinno
Design: BermanLaVO *bermanlavo.com*

Dedicated to

Bryce, Paige, Hailey, and Nathan
My children who are the loves of my life

TABLE OF CONTENTS

ACKNOWLEDGEMENTS

I'd like to start by thanking my husband, Craig Hunter for being my sweetheart and giving me the encouragement and space needed to produce this work of the heart which can only come from a foundation of love. Craig enriches my life every day with three beautiful angels, Chasen, Olivia and Logan. I love each and every one of you.

To my very best friend / soul sister, Sheri a.k.a. 'Pips' Hammer, where do I begin? Thirty-Eight years and counting, you have been there for me every single day. You have been my laughter, my tears and my support when I needed it most. There are no words to express the depth of our friendship which to my way of thinking is eternal. I love the bee-jeezus out of you :)

Christine Carlo, your nudge as a 'You have to do this!' was the reason I considered writing this book. The determination to see this work realized and checking in to make sure I was actually doing this – was essential to manifesting what was inside me all along. I love you.

Norah Wynne, a.k.a. 'Four' you have been such a huge part of this journey, thank you for all the support and for believing in me. I will forever hold dear the countless hours of laughter and tears we have shared together in writing this book. Your kind patronage made this personal expression to the world possible. I love you.

Of course, there is my mother and father, Gary and Linda Cunningham without whom I wouldn't be on the planet. You have always been there for me no matter what. My endless gratitude goes to you both for always encouraging me patiently and without judgement, allowing me to be who I am to figure out my own way to live. Your grace was what gave me the space to blossom. Daddy, I feel you with me every day. I love you both.

Kim Roth. Where would I be today if you had not been my advocate at Strength United? You were my rock and now you are a part of my family. Thank you for believing in me and never giving up on me. You have lifted me higher than I could have ever imagined. Now I can fly! I love you.

Jane Creighton, thank you for being an instrument to my freedom. Your commitment to see the truth make its way to the surface is what brings light and peace for so many people. I could not have done it without you. You are a Rock Star in my world. I love you.

Julie Hemingway-Keitz, you are my 'TRUE-BLUE' Julie! You opened the door. You rolled out the red carpet (*literally because my yoga mat you gave me was red*) on the journey to myself. I am grateful for your strength, courage and compassion. You were there for me to hold the pieces when I didn't know how I was going to put myself back together again. I love you.

To all the good people at Strength United, I am indebted to your ability to see beyond the violence and into the souls of people like me. You saved my life. May God protect you and carry you so that you may continue to be the refuge, provide sanctuary and save the lives of so many. You are the bodhisattvas on this planet. I love you.

To my soul brother, mentor and teacher, Tony Di Zinno. Our journey together in laughter, tears, chest-bumps, inside jokes, *(honk-honk)* and happy-dancing will always be one of the great treasures of my heart. You have taught me so much, not only about writing but about myself. Your humility cracked opened the places where I previously had doubts, so that I could share my story in this authentic voice. I love you. Namaste b.

Shana Berger, a.k.a. 'Shanah-bah-nah-nah'! Thank you for always grounding me and holding space in a way like no other. Your loyalty and commitment to our friendship is and forever will be precious to me. I love you.

Mary Church, a.k.a. "Lama-mama' you've always reminded me and encouraged me to stand on top of the mountain of my own stories. I have cherished your way of always seeing the strength and independence in me. Takes one to know one. I love you.

Dolby Dubrow, aka 'Lillith'. Hot, gorgeous and profane! You are the trumpet of what is true. Loud and proud, yet tender and peaceful. Always on the right side of things. Thank you for reminding me that I am a Phoenix rising out of the ashes into the sky. I love you.

To my 'Tama-lama', you know who you are! You protected me and loyally stood by my side during the most devastating time of my life, . . . and you loved me anyway. Thank you forever. I love you.

Brett Moisa, you were the one who kept us safe and risked your own welfare to help us in a time of crisis. You have been my friend for so many years. We have shared many stories together. Thank you for being there when I needed you most. I love you.

Thanks to God.
I bow to you.
I love you.

FOREWARD

*J*ulie Hunter has offered us a precious gift. She tells of the shocking death of her first husband and she describes in unflinching detail the humiliating abuse she suffered for five years at the hands of a monstrous man.

A high percentage of the people I have seen in my 40 years of practice as a clinical psychologist have experienced trauma. The inclination of so many is to tell no one, to keep it secret especially if it is the kind of abuse Julie experienced. So often when someone tries to bury past trauma it becomes toxic. The sense of shame which may develop can lead to depression, addiction and illness.

That's why Julie's book is so important. She holds nothing back as she details the devastating abuse she experienced. There is great power in simple and complete openness and honesty. It's as if she is saying to the reader, "I'm taking you into my confidence hoping that it may help you to know what I went through and how I survived."

But this is much more than the story of her survival, this is the story of her personal empowerment. She takes us with her on her spiritual and philosophical journey to replenishment.

I met Julie as my Yoga teacher before I knew anything about her past. Since I know her personally I can say that she has become a warm, lovely, joyful woman. She is flourishing.

Dr. Warren Walker
Clinical Psychologist

Hope

PREFACE
My wound is my grace.

 $\mathcal{T}$ hat's my intention in this book.

It's what I'm supposed to be doing.

There is a spirit embracing both of us that acts as an invitation to grace. The magic is coming into awareness together. Maybe our hearts are opening a little bit more today than they did only yesterday. Once we have finally surrendered, and willingly entered into the wound purposely, the alignment with grace becomes a natural way of being.

As an activist of peace... I believe peace starts at home. In everything we do, I aim in keeping with all things sacred to hold the highest form of integrity and honesty in this work. Now, I wake up and think, "What do I want to learn today?"

Therefore, this is what I'll teach.

I have been going through this interesting roller coaster where I had to give myself permission to be seriously angry. Yes. I gave myself permission to be really angry.

Pain is a funny thing.
When you're trying to survive, pain is something that you want to put aside because it blinds you from being clear and from doing the right thing, ... however it's still there. We tend to want to either avoid it or get rid of it by projecting it onto somebody else.

What to do about this *it* thing?

What I do now as a matter of my best practice is to strive for a deeper understanding of myself and what I can do to change ... it. I've realized that I'm an empath. When an empath is in a relationship with a sociopath, the line gets very diffused and we take a lot of stuff on that doesn't belong to us. I began to wonder if there are a lot of women that have been subjected to domestic violence that are empaths as well. Even as a yoga instructor, when I talk about moving the body or the breath, finding the asana, so to speak, it's about integrating everything.

I once read a beautiful quote by Dr. Lauren Deville that describes the process of unreleased pain..

"The body weeps tears that eyes cannot shed"

I'm learning to listen more to my body as a yoga practitioner. There has been tremendous pain throughout my own physical and emotional practice, yet I often felt that suffering equals weakness because I could not afford to be hurt anymore. I had to be strong. Even throughout the days of living in violence I did not show my anguish. To expose my fear and to fall apart made me out to be a target for more abuse. At the time, I simply didn't understand what pain was nor the value of it. Our misery becomes the enemy, especially when its misunderstood.

There was never any arguing within my home growing up, it was forbidden. It was only later in life that I learned pain and suffering would become useful companions. Now, I don't prefer to get rid of the pain as much as I choose to process it and listen to the tormenter in disguise as the loving teacher it has appeared to be in my life.

It is with great confidence I can say this because I have been in situations where the sting of suffering has led me to actually find more wisdom in myself. The affliction itself has been the driving force to figure out who I really am. Sometimes it creeps in and builds up and you think you're over something and done.

Guess what? You are not done yet.

Damn it! I thought I was over this!

Congratulations you are in turmoil!

This is great because, you're ready to figure something else out that is even better about yourself. Mind you, it doesn't always feel that way when you're in the shit. For example, these days when anger is ramping up inside of me and what feels like an overload of conflict going on around me … it's a perfect sign of the confusion for me to recognize.

Am I ready for a reality check?

I don't throw things or consciously choose to hurt myself and others when I'm outraged. But when I'm heated, my unconscious attempts to refuse the anger through avoidance is the actual thing that is hurting me. The great lesson here is, there is no way to hurt yourself without harming others. If we choose to shut down or be unkind to ourselves this radiates throughout our entire being and is what we have left to offer to others.

What do I do with this energy?

Instead of turning away, because that is what I would habitually do – I am more conscious of it – I can sit and look at it because I know it has the right to be there, otherwise it wouldn't have shown up. When we say, "I have the right to be angry!", we also may admit for the first time that our anger, rage, and jealousy also have the authority to make an appearance. These feelings are one way your authentic self has of telling you, "Hello sweetheart! Boy are you confused!" Don't you realize you have a choice? You can feed me, by grasping and ignore me or we can sit together for a moment and investigate.

Let's be honest, shall we?

When anger comes to visit our house, it can be like a traveling salesman, wait - what?

DING DONG!

I didn't ask for this!
How about you answer the door for me?

I'll take out the trash! Don't tell them I'm here!

I now learn to consciously say, "OK, I remember you and that's all right come on in…" *(sometimes with a little pout on my face)*. One of the most significant ways I was getting through my experience of PTSD, was by facing up to the pain instead of trying to get away from it. Picture this; I literally laid myself out on the floor and said, "Come on now, … I feel you, I hear you, do what you need to do bitches!"

BRING IT ON.

I would start to focus on my physical body where I notice the sensations and breathing through it. Keeping in mind that violence creates more violence. The secrets harbor the violence. Therefore, I no longer held the secret of my anger from myself. When feeling discomfort and irritation then choosing to push it away, I am actually creating more chaos. Now, I'm drawing even more insanity into my life whether I'm aware of it or not.

It's been a great learning process and it always will be, no longer the villain to be avoided. It has evolved into a great teacher for me when the provenance presents itself. To write this book and start reliving these stories is almost like going into an attic where I had forgotten the things I have stored away years ago. Dusting these stories off gave me the chance to go deeper into myself than I have ever been before.

Visiting ourselves in this way is a sweet kind of homecoming. It's like the unveiling of the mirrors that no longer give a proper reflection of who we understand ourselves to be today. Clarity comes from understanding, knowing, and alignment with the source of who you are. That begs the question who the fuck are you?

Open the windows. Let the light in again. Reconsider the old stories in the attic of your head.
Opening the doors of perception are instrumental to the encountering of our sanity, like nectar from the mouth of God speaking truth to you. It is nothing less than my opportunity for everything that I want good in this life. The offer is the source of either staying in the wound of wisdom or to get lost in the illusion of its violent, daunting and frightening appearance.

Whether it's interpersonal conflict or a clash between countries, I do believe everything regarding global suffering stems from our wounds of wisdom or the lack of understanding the wisdom of these wounds. If we inflict this suffering every day on ourselves *(in our own heads)* how can we expect the world outside of us to be any different?

My story doesn't consist of being a third world refugee or a prisoner of war with bombs going off all around me. I don't live in the same places where the common practice of pulling women onto the streets to be stoned to death is still tolerated. My reality included a more personal conflict zone right at home. Being on the wrong end of a series of ass-kickings behind closed doors was my day to day private hell.

I humbly come to this project knowing that there's far more work to be done for all of us. I'm hoping somehow this book will touch on something everyone can relate to. Like a groovy rhythm, it's calling us to move our souls together in harmony of a familiar tune -welcoming us back home. Maybe, the big idea is for us to see things for what they really are - instead of what they appear to be. Then, we all have a stronger sense of an authentic self.
Dance to your own rhythm.
When we become entangled in the illusions and hide behind the secrets of shame and guilt, we lose sight as to how we are going to free ourselves. We are inundated with dreaded thoughts of 'how in the hell am I going to get out of this?' These fleeting thoughts flood in faster than we can even deal with them in any rational way.

I'm screwed!

I am going to die.

He is going kill me.

He will hurt my children.

He will take my children away.

Why am I still here? How did I get here?

What is it that keeps me imprisoned in this situation? I know for myself I had to have a personal reckoning with my part in it when before I was only focused on the other. I consider myself a compassionate human being. How could that possibly bring me any suffering? The truth is there is a downside even to things we look to as virtues. For example, I am empathic. We tend to romanticize empaths. This is where we all get messed up... at least I did. The reality is, this gift is both a blessing and a curse.

Is it possible we are all getting confused about how good intentions can complicate the very thing that we are trying to be a solution for? It is tricky and sticky. Empaths look to others suffering and pain because they are provoked by the massive discomfort it makes them feel when their sensitivities are already on the next level.

The danger here is a temptation to go where angels dare not tread. A misguided sense of self-esteem can be witnessed in the trespassing of boundaries when sensing another's pain. Imposing or interfering with another's dignity to their own sacred path is 'none of our business'. Just because we see or feel their torment does not make it ours to fix, or pluck the lesson it holds for them.

When it appears someone is willing to hurt so much for us, it subconsciously relieves our constant avoidance of our responsibility. You are hurting. Now, I am hurting and can't stand that. Clearly, I have to do something about it. To make someone else's agony ours by taking it on when it is not even ours to begin with, will always end up amplifying the misery. Some may confuse empath with martyrdom.

Why is martyrdom so attractive?

The key here is the unconscious empath always finds themselves in a relationship where the pain is the main attraction. It gives us a false sense of importance, of love and purpose.

Sometimes we resign ourselves.

When the feeling comes over me that I am falling to pieces and I am aware of it …
I give myself the time I need. When I'm ready to put myself back together again-
that's when I take action. This is very nuanced if only it provides me the pause to
sit, reflect and place myself in the gap.

What is this Gap thing you ask?
The *gap* is the space between thoughts, feelings and action. It is most easily
accessed in moments of meditation. Looking inward and watching my breath
move in and out of the body is one way that I find myself in the gap. For me, it's
the time and space needed to move from the familiar into the possibility of a new
frontier of unknown ways of being. It's like a resting place.

I don't want to be that old shape and form anymore. My choice is to be a willing
part of the transformation, not a hostage to it. Once I am willing to change my
mind, therein lies the path to transition my life.

When I witness these negative emotions that feel like a juggernaut coming down
the rails, my poor self, shouts, "Where is my hero to save the day and cut the
ropes binding me to my one track mind"?

Sorry, … ain't no hero coming, sweetheart!
It's just you and the train. What are you going to do about it? What can I do? I'm
tied to the track. I'm helpless, right? Or am I really? Is this how it ends for me? Do
I die in this version of my story?

Is this story even real …or am I in a dream?

It's not until I pause and step outside the story that I can hear the painful truth
of an inner wisdom that I have been resisting. Perhaps, I may be the one casting
myself into the role of damsel in distress - or hero to the rescue. Is it possible that
I was never the victim at all?

Am I willing to even consider the notion that it was me who was the villain (*in
disguise*) all along binding myself to the thoughts that have kept me in the role of
the victim? This awareness saved my life. I embraced the opportunity to challenge
the previous narrative, change the story and recast myself as a new character.
Nothing real was binding me in the first place… just my beliefs.

Once I found myself in the precious state of resignation, all the worn out beliefs
that once held me fast to this track were loosened … there was now enough
movement to slip out from the bonds and free myself. I had finally found the
courage to be released from my self-made traps.

Change

INTRODUCTION
A bona fide writer.

*E*ven after a year of writing this book and watching it come to fruition, I'm still not ready to admit that I am a real writer at all. I never claimed to be. The intention behind the writing of this book was not to gain recognition as a scholar or be seen as the kind of woman who claims to know anything more *(or less)* than anyone else. My primary motive comes from the desire to share a life of profound personal experiences and a deep abiding love of the truth.

Today, I am a liberator and a survivor.

With enough courage, I've overcome the illusions of whom I thought I was previously. I'm learning to humbly stumble through the process of being a novice, if only to share my story with the world in the hopes that it may be helpful to those who read this book and might use it as an inspiration. That would be an elegant outcome.

The people we choose for our personal relationships and the families we grow up with operate within a matrix of perceptions and beliefs we have about ourselves, as the result of these stories of origin. We cast our own personal set of villains and heroes, even our loved ones become the supporting characters in the dramas of our lives. Although it may be hard to believe, all of our experiences of the past, have nothing to do with who we are today.

Some of our stories are hopefully filled with laughter, joy and even ecstasy, while other narratives may haunt us with violence and grief. If we choose to be in the painful past and allow it to transform our reality and hold us captive - we will always be searching for a life story that fits into the puzzle pieces of our suffering.

We have two worlds we live in.
The first is the private and powerful world of the heart. The other is what appears

to be the so called real world as we experience the exterior of the body and the physical. At the end of the day we are not our stories nor do they exist in any concrete way anywhere but within our limited thought space.

Whom we choose to be during life ... is ultimately up to each one of us.

When we become aware of the difference between what our memories hold for us and the labels we place upon them, we then have the space to choose what feels right and wrong. The truth is everywhere and it shows itself to those that dare to consider how loved they truly are. We live in a world filled with make believe stories all around us each and every day. Who is to say which ones are real and which ones aren't real?
(hint: only you do!)

We are all holders of a divine intelligence with the ability to recognize not only the truth but feel the love that created it. I have come to discover that whenever I feel terrified or unsure of myself or others, it is just the voice of wisdom calling me back home. The experiences we fear most are an excellent opportunity for us to recognize our internal compass broadcasting where freedom and truth can be found.

We tend to look to other people and their views of us to help define our sense of greatness or unworthiness. The relationships we seek are a direct reflection of our own beliefs about the person we subconsciously have come to believe ourselves to be. This is a most unkind trick we play against ourselves. Personally, I have not always lived in an environment of harmony and joy. In fact, it has at times been quite physically violent and terrifying.

The absolute conviction of my own stories of the past had once confined me to a mental prison with bars built with shame, guilt and fear. I will never claim to know what it is like to be anyone other than myself. Further, I have genuine respect for all those that choose to own up to their own lives. I'm grateful for those that share their truth so that the entire world can be somehow touched and awakened by their stories.

We may observe ourselves as collective beings who have been given the great gift of relating to one another and offering our understanding and compassion to others – but only when it's available as a gift bestowed to us as individuals first.

I can't help but believe that we all as spiritual beings in these human bodies have a choice to show up within our own unique and beautiful lives any way we choose. It can be disheartening to think for just a moment that we are not the free spirits we came here to be. Some people say it is impossible to be happy after experiencing tragedy and abuse. There are too many of us that feel trapped and helpless when it comes to imagining we could ever be happy again. I too have felt myself imprisoned without a glimpse of hope waiting for me on the horizon.

Why do some people get to be happy while others suffer?

Is this how it is supposed to be? Are there only a certain hand-picked few that pull the long straw of happiness while the others get the short end of the stick? For decades, I believed I was an unlucky and helpless victim in this world. Ironically, it wasn't until I was imprisoned by a violent man, ritually beaten and raped for years that I was willing to see myself as someone different.

If you have picked up this book and will allow me to share my story with you, there is a good chance you are ready to see yourself as someone different too. I want you to know that I believe with all my heart and soul, we have the capacity to be happy and free. It will be up to us to do the work of self -exploration and internal investigation - - or not.

There is nothing anyone outside of us can do to keep us away from the truth of our own inner voice and our path to empowerment. Just know that we are and always will be free to make a choice. This opportunity never expires and it is patiently waiting ... respecting our own personal timing. It doesn't care about the past or even the future. It has no conditions and no scorecard to fill.
We are not alone nor has another ever abandoned us. It may appear that way sometimes but our willingness to take ownership of our lives and the way we believe ourselves to be liberated in it - is optional. May we always be patient and kind to ourselves throughout this exciting journey of "self-discovery" and remember we are not alone.

The truth is, we are all free to come up with our own beautiful conclusions based on this ultimately personal transformative experience.

Self-Realization

CHAPTER 1
Who is this relationship about anyway?

*W*ho do you love?

Who do you hate?

Who is this relationship about anyway?

Think about all of the people we have crossed paths with and shared our deepest most intimate parts of ourselves with. The list becomes very interesting. When we think about the ones we use to love … do we still love them? Have we outgrown them or have they outgrown us? Some of us may giggle to think of the embarrassment of a past relationship. Perhaps you have been betrayed and scarred for life with the painful memory of being deceived.

Do you still love that person?

Maybe you have changed your mind about your affections towards them and they become an enemy. How can we love and hate the same person in one lifetime? We are masters at looking outward for reasons to love and for reasons to hate. Who does it make us when we choose one over the other? If we continue to see ourselves through the eyes of what another person believes, then who in the hell are WE?

Believing ourselves as a prisoner of someone else's opinions of us is to my way of thinking completely insane! It can be through the idea of love or even hate. Why do we insist that someone else has the power to decipher and determine our existence? Why would we think someone other than ourselves is responsible for our sense of happiness or grief? To please us becomes their job eventually becoming one of the essential parts of our own identity.

I shall be served.

This is a vulnerable and dangerous place to be because the fabric can only hold you for so long before it begins to tear. Do we like having the responsibility for another human being's welfare all day, ... every day? If you are saying yes, then take a moment to reflect on your genuine respect and love for that person, better yet check in with your sense of self-respect. If we find pleasure in vengeance and vindictiveness, then be prepared for the other person to not give a damn. Then you are stuck with yourself and all of the rising tide of discomfort of your own self-reflective perceptions of them.

When we continue to lie to ourselves and shut off from the intimacy that waits to be recognized - - we shall suffer. This love-hate relationship that we continue to generate is with us and in fact ... is us! There is no other out there that makes you feel or experience anything. If we love it is because the other makes us feel wonderful and happy. When we hate ... it is because the other has wronged us in some way that makes us feel terrible and vengeful.

Why do we give ourselves away so easily?

Anytime I would rack my brain with this theory the answer stays the same. I feel things. Then I notice what I feel ... and see the other does the same within their own experience. We get blindsided when our partner decides to take their love and share it with another person, because we were under the impression of possessing their love – totally.

"How could you do such a horrible thing to me!"

The power we give away to others unwittingly can be crippling and even catastrophic to our sense of well-being. I have lived with this concept for most of my life and throughout all of the heartache and pain, I have noticed something undeniable - I am left alone. Was I not alone before? Did I grow an arm or a leg with this partner and not even realize it? Who was I when I wasn't betrayed or beat up? Who am I now that my partner has made his own choices with and without me?

When my practice of meditation became a daily experience, much confusion about the Julie I believed myself to be transformed in a way that did not include anyone else in the definition.

Yes, it really is all about me!

When I choose to be happy, sad, loved, hated, thrown away for another I am still left with Julie. Dear God, what a discovery! Who was going to give me a purpose and significance in this world? Will I even exist if another doesn't see me the way I want them to? How in the hell was I going to put that responsibility onto another when I didn't even have the awareness myself?

To look into the eyes of another person and tell them you love them is a lie if you don't recognize the love you have for yourself first.

We cannot give something away if we don't realize that we possess it in the first place. Instead, we tell our partners, "I love you because I have chosen you to be the love that I don't know how to recognize in myself." If you choose to leave me, I will hate you forever for robbing me of my happiness!" This is crazy making - yet this is what we do to one another. No one teaches us this stuff when we are growing up because no one taught the previous generation before us.
How cruel to place such rationale on another and what a lie it is to say you love them at the same time. Intimacy is a personal relationship between you and yourself.

"IN-TO-ME-SEES!" *(get it?)*

Whoever rattles our cage becomes the significant and most vital teachers we could ever ask for. What have we forgotten about our own beauty and self-worth?

We can't give away our love when we aren't even awake to what it means in the first place. Have you ever noticed the days when nothing pleases you and everyone is pissing you off?

Then suddenly a partner who lights your fire appears in your life and wants to share their undying love with you. Nothing appears grim on that day. You are loved and you can be reassured that you matter to someone that *'rocks your world'*!

Same daily routine, yet everything is suddenly - so wonderful! Did this stranger withhold some kind of magic wand from me for all of these years? What did I do to deserve this windfall of goodness? Why couldn't I be this happy before this new love came into my life? Is it because I too have the one and only magic wand they have been looking for as well? Nonsense.
To be intimate with the self is where it will start, stop and everything in between.

"IN-TO-ME-MATE" *(written with tongue firmly in cheek).*

This is the perfect partner. The love. The fear. Trust and hope is all up to you. Imagine what incredible relationships we can share once we have awakened from the nightmare of someone else's dream of us . . . and us of them.
At times, I look back to the partners I have chosen in my life and where I would be today if we were still together. I take a giant sigh of relief when I think of the bullet I've dodged, literally! No matter how insane the experiences seem to me now, I thank each and every one of them for showing up and fulfilling their promise consciously or unconsciously. The relationships were our sacred calling

4

to one another so we could get to know our selves better.

We do not see others for who they are ... Rather, it's more like we see others for who we are! When playing the victim, we are not able to nurture the true sense of self. Isn't that absolutely fabulous to know this? Maybe? Maybe not! However, it can be the first step towards the greatest most exciting adventure of your life - the love and eternal friendship between you and your higher self! There is nothing more transcendent and joyful than that. What a great way to experience ourselves when we can share this realization with others.

Letting Go

CHAPTER 2
Just how naïve was I then?

$\mathcal{I}$ had been going through the pained confusion of a troubled and terminal marriage to my high school sweetheart, Charles. Charlie, my first husband was impossibly handsome. He was so good looking that he made James Dean look like puppy chow. *(NOTE: no movie stars were harmed in the making of this book).* My beloved was vibrant and full of life when we met. My blissfully innocent self couldn't begin to fathom what rabbit holes we were going down. In terms of consequences, everything he did was always done to the maximum extreme.

Charles lived his life to the fullest in all his pursuits from his partying to excelling in every sport. After graduating high school, he went into the military where he naturally became an elite U.S. Army Ranger. All I knew was how to endure, raise four kids and go with the flow of moving to new places and having to start all over again. My goal was to be the most loving wife I could be.

After 17 years of adventure, things with Charlie began to unravel. There were signs of his mental health coming apart at the seams. It got so bad between us that despite the fact we had our four children together, we agreed to a separation – at least for a time. There were lots of rumors around the neighborhood about Charlie's supposed crystal meth abuse. While I didn't even know what crystal-meth was, I did notice his previously world class chiseled physique had diminished to the point where he was terribly thin and had an open sore on the right side of his face.

I didn't know where that mark came from.

He wouldn't show up for work anymore. He was complaining of tingling in his fingers and toes. One of the last times I saw him was when he was climbing so slowly up the stairs that he was literally a shadow of his former self. He was a man being ravaged by addiction. Soon came the fear, paranoia and the unwelcome presence of a loaded firearm in the house.

What's worse than a train wreck?

My life with Charlie was more like a shipwreck waiting to happen. You know, the kind where you can see it coming from a long ways off . . . as if it is in slow motion yet all the yelling and screaming in the world still can't stop it. If there ever was such a thing as a personal warning beacon in the form of a kind of lighthouse for me to navigate by - my life was being lived in the dark. I mean to say the predominant feeling was nothing but surging waves of emotion and the abyss below of an impossibly rocky landing waiting for us as a family.

One of the hallmarks in my experience of grave mental health problems like addiction, is to witness a remarkable sense of self-absorption in the afflicted to the exclusion of everything else. Love, affection and responsibility all took a back seat to the never-ending striving for the next distraction. What I learned from this was the profound lesson of:

> *'the temporary interruption of unhappiness is*
> *not ever to be confused with real happiness.'*

I was literally a woman starved for affection. My body was painfully thin at the time because the stress was overwhelming. This was a sign that things were not right with my interior life despite what the trappings and glamour on the outside looked like. You can put the most elegant trendy brands to dress up in ... but there is a world of difference between being fashionably thin and then beginning to show signs of something more serious going on.

My girlfriends were obviously concerned and saw fit to invite me out to the posh Twin Palms in Santa Clarita. A night out with the women was a very rare thing. It was a once in a blue moon occasion to go somewhere without kids and get together with three of my old high school gal pals. I felt like a fish out of water and didn't know what to do with myself. Everything else around me was falling apart.

Then the man whom I would never marry *(but my future would be tied to for years)* showed up to this gathering and fatefully approached our table. This unannounced stranger was full to the brim with all the swagger of a gunslinger. He quickly picked up the chair next to me and spun it around as if he had choreographed his first impression. Mick cut a charming figure and he knew it. I mean, he really bounced when he walked!

"Pleased to meet you ... can you guess my name?"
At first glance, Mick didn't strike me as someone I would be that into. Looking back, I thought little of his canned introduction. Remember, I was the one who was

having babies and been married since I was 18 years old. I was not accustomed to having men as friends that I could hang out with.

Here I was, facing the ongoing tragedy of watching my husband disappear from me bit by painful bit through his struggle with mental illness and addiction. I admit I was intrigued by Mick's ability to make me laugh and ease the pain I was experiencing at the time.

Charles had become alarmingly depressed to a point where we felt our lives were no longer safe in his presence. He had struggled with drugs and alcohol throughout our entire marriage, yet he had an amazing side to him that for everyone that knew him eclipsed anything else.

Everybody loved Charlie. He was a beautiful man full of life and vigor, yet he harbored a tremendous rage inside and a frightening disposition when he was triggered.

There was no saving Charlie from himself. The paranoia became so much a part and parcel of his drug use that he seized upon this new acquaintance of mine. In Mick, he saw someone to be insanely jealous of. His inner demons soon took over his mind. I had removed the gun from the house when I found it fully loaded with six bullets... make no mistake that is one for each member of our struggling family. People who loved Charlie could not - or would not - believe me when I tried to convince them the loaded gun was evidence of Charlie's potential ambivalence.

I was out of the house on an errand when our daughter Paige who was 12 at the time, called to say her Dad, (Charlie) had left a note for me in the garage and then left. He had up ended an entire ping-pong table and flipped it over to use the unpainted bottom to write me a sort of ultimatum note. In black marker pen, he wrote his last letter to me on the wooden underside. In the note he mentions, he won't see me ever again – that he was leaving the country and that I could keep the house. Also, he said that he loved me and the kids more than life itself. The message so disturbed me I couldn't sleep. In the wee hours, I rang my friend Tami to share with her about it.

I was in a state of shock and didn't know what to make of this . . .

On that call, while talking to Tami I had a premonition of his death. It was an intense and immediate panic sensation. I remember coming to a complete halt in the conversation because my body was feeling extremely hot and cold at the same time. Standing in the garage reading his good-bye note, I shouted to Tami on the other end of the line, "Oh my God – Charlie is dead! I felt him cross over just now!"

I felt it.

I was trembling and I couldn't breathe.

Tami, ... Charlie is gone!"

Pain. Severity. Certainty. It was done.

Even though I had that indescribable knowing not everyone else was convinced. Being so close with someone over seventeen years provides for the kind of spiritual connection that can give us glimpses into things that are otherwise unseen or unknowable. People were waiting for him to resurface. He never did. We wouldn't find his body for another fourteen days ...

It was only just a few short weeks after I met Mick that my poor husband took his own life. Charlie had found an isolated place in the woods and took himself out with CO2 poisoning using the exhaust of his truck to end his suffering in this existence. Two women on a motorcycle rode passed his truck and stopped to investigate because they noticed the unmistakable signature of death and decay where the one of a kind smell in nature, signals the certainty of the result with a taste of copper metallic lingering in one's mouth.

The world I knew came to a complete halt and I was no longer in a place where I could make a clear decision - let alone defend myself for his choice to end his life.

This one took me to my knees...

People were already quick to blame me for his earlier disappearance. It was apparent to me that I was going to be the one ending up getting the blame for Charlie's death and the insanity of that thought alone put me in a state of pure panic and uncertainty. Over the following days and nights, I noticed things started to go missing from our garage as if it was open season for looters. A free for all for poachers, predators and people pilfering our life. It was as if the home we had made together with Charlie was itself mortally wounded and the hyenas were picking over the carcass of our life.

My children and I no longer felt safe in our own home.

Mick was there for me *(and my kids)* and he was also the reason people wrongly blamed me for the tragedy. My children and I huddled up wanting to get as far away from the chaos as possible. Mick wanted to take us all in ... and be the hero.

I made a choice to be rescued and feel safe regardless of what my inner voice was calling me to hear. Only months into the aftermath of my husband, Mick asked me to marry him. It wasn't like we discussed it or anything. He couldn't wait to make us a family. He had his own needs. Yes, he had shown great love and compassion to my children and me. That's about all I had in the world to hang onto at that time. I handed the steering wheel of my life over to a complete stranger whom I hadn't even previously been dating.

When I look back now, I think what the fuck was I thinking? Yet, I honestly believed at the time that I had nowhere else to turn. Money was never the issue as I was financially taken care of, yet, all onlookers wanted to believe it was Mick's prosperity that was the main attraction for me. It was more about the physical and emotional safety I found in Mick because he was always there for me as an incredibly attentive listener.

What woman wouldn't welcome that?

He was patient, loving and kind. We had the ability to laugh and explore life in a way I never knew before. The more time that passed I sincerely thought I was falling in love and felt that I had found a deep and meaningful connection to this man. Truth be told, ... I was in too much of a tumult to know what was the right thing for me to do during this time of personal maelstrom.

The pain was completely taking me over.

With the perspective of hindsight, I can look back through the fog I was navigating at the time and see more realistically the jeopardy I was putting myself into. I knew that if I faced this grief of Charlie's suicide alone I wasn't going to make it – not even a few days on my own. One vivid memory is when I would go to bed at night and feel heavy pressure on my chest to the point where I felt I couldn't breathe. My fear of not waking up in the morning had me convinced my body would somehow forget how to draw air into my lungs and I would simply die in my sleep.

I couldn't find my way home within myself.

My own pain was incomprehensible. The people whom I thought were my trusted confidantes and claimed to be my friends chose to make it more about themselves. Their grief. Their confusion. Even the local sheriff took interested random people up on a field trip to tour the suicide scene like it was a morbid sideshow attraction.

I felt like I had been raped.

The whole town was caught up in glamorizing the sad story. Everyone seemed to want to be a victim of it and believe they were the ones suffering the most. Like it was a kind of competition for those who were the most affected. I shut myself out from all of them. Aftershocks in this small town could be felt in the ripple effect from ground zero. Even at the funeral, more than half the people wouldn't even look at me.

The shunning was horrible.

The aftermath of a suicide in a small town like this can act like a virus. Literally, it is a corrupting influence on the morals and or the intellects as if the town's water supply had been poisoned. It can send a town like ours into disarray when people are so caught up in gossiping and the destructive one-upmanship in terms of competing for the significance of their pain. When shame and guilt overwhelm us we end up hating ourselves. The guilt was intense. It's like a sting ... I am still trying to soften around it.

Sudden resignation...

There was the resignation of my broken family. The entire town was in a frenzy. Everyone hurried to do something out of a pure fucking emotional panic. Had the world gone nuts? Wildly unthinking behavior was the order of the day. Charlie and I were widely seen in our hamlet as the perfect couple. Perhaps the terrible thought that occurred to folks was if it happened to Charlie and Julie – it can happen to any of us! Charlie's suicide rocked the foundation of the community. This busted open the small-town vanity of how something as taboo as self-annihilation could never happen to people like us.

Arrogance.

Ignorance.

This hit close to the bone for Frazier Park.
Mick became a hero to those in my circle that wanted to believe he loved us so much that he would heroically be willing to take on a widow and her four children. He showered me with beautiful things and showed me new landscapes my eyes had never seen before. I soon found myself surrounded by new faces and new places.

This was indeed a massive distraction and gave my mind an opportunity to get a break from the shock and grief. Despite the extrication from my tumult, I noticed with each passing day I did not get better but became more and more dysfunctional. Mick would pick up the pieces and give me a chance to recover - or so it seemed. Wow. What a great guy. What an amazing man! This was the mantra we spoke over and over to ourselves as a distraction from the ugly truth of what was really happening.

It wasn't too long after the kids and I settled into a new home with Mick - which in hindsight was a massive mistake - that the kids started to inform me of strange behavior they had been witnessing from him. They would report to me that he would listen at the door while I was on the phone and he would treat them differently when I wasn't around. Mick began to monitor my calendar and take over my ability to make my own decisions and justify this because of the impairment due to my grief process.

He soon wiggled his insane reasoning into my head that I was not capable of making any good choices, that I needed to start to see things in a "better" way. He was the voice of reason and I was not. He made it clear I needed to trust him more. Mick reminded me often of the bad marriage that had damaged my ability to know what was right for my kids and myself. Around this time, he insisted the children refer to him as their 'Dad'.

My girlfriends were receiving phone calls from Mick informing them as to when I was to be home and where I was allowed to go. My friends became concerned when he would repeat private phone conversations that he had not been a participant in. The discomfort and fear started to become more frequent as Mick would holler and drag me out of the vehicle when my friends would drop me off after a girl's evening out. At first it was the hard squeezes on my arms. Then, as things escalated, it would be a twist with a pull, accompanied by verbal threats born out of insecurity that were illustrating what would become an emerging pattern of serious agitation.The arguing became more frequent and turned into a daily experience. The stresses on Mick not being able to control me were taking a toll on him and he was going to make sure I paid the price for his displeasure. He soon escalated from the pedestrian violence into our first full body slam straight to the ground on the floor of our bedroom.

This was Mick's way of making clear who was in charge and what the consequences would be if I upset him. He screamed, "How could you do this to me?" It was his reason for being in such distress. You see, ... I was being convinced of being this horrible person who had no real understanding of love.

I found myself not believing what was really happening. I could not for the life of me figure out what I was doing that was so bad. I wanted to be my own person and I knew I was a woman that wanted desperately to offer a 'normal' and healthy life to my family. My children deserved to be in a home with love and stability and I couldn't wrap my mind around what was happening with his choice of behavior.

Following our first physical blow out Mick would follow up his violence upon me with a honeymoon stage rich with the tears and apologies, including declarations of love that led us to couples counseling in hopes of creating something healthier than where we were at the time. Therapy became the crutch Mick would lean on to keep me in the relationship with promises of a "better future" after each violent argument.

This became a kind of mantra for Mick.

The more time we passed as a couple the longer the gaps were between these cease-fire moments of contrition and polite begging for going to couples therapy. It was becoming evident how narcissistic Mick was to see how he would try to convince me it was somehow my fault that he pushed me to the ground.

There was a manipulation where Mick suggested the loss of Charlie was causing me not to see things the right way - which of course was his way. Because of the state of mind I was in, I mistakenly took his overreactions for a kind of romantic charge in our high intensity relationship. There must be something there if sparks are flying, right? I didn't confide in anyone about this escalation. I didn't need any "I told you so's" either. There was already enough shame to go around.

I started to question my ability to make a so-called 'right' decision on everything I was doing. I asked myself if I was asleep for my whole life before Mick because I became confused about my ability to make a good choice. There was never a day when I wasn't lectured on how badly I hurt him or let him down. I was slowly losing myself because everything was about his wants, his needs and how he wanted to be loved.

The remarkable thing about my life at this point was to look back on Mick's near total negation of my right to make my own friends, to come and go as I pleased or even be a mother to my grieving children. It wasn't long before I realized how jealous he was of the times I spent with my kids.

How long can one abandon oneself before one is lost?

Against my better judgment, I reverently worked on bettering myself and trying to see things his way. The black hole of this intractable relationship began to open and suck me into it bit by bit. Things were happening too fast to even deal with it. It was all I could do to stay afloat.

The experience of a person screwing with my head wasn't something that had ever happened to me before. It was incomprehensible to me at the time. I was the sort of naïve person who always trusted the good intentions of others right from the start. I wanted to believe what I wanted to believe and rejected the reality of what Mick was actually doing to me. He reminded me daily that he would never feel this angry if he didn't love me so much. Who was I to hurt another person when all they wanted to do was love me?

Deep within me, I knew something wasn't right - yet the fear and confusion was the choice I made over the wisdom of my soul.

Unconditional Love

CHAPTER 3
What I believed

$\mathcal{I}$ once heard someone say that captivity is a mentality. We take these beliefs with us everywhere we go. Three years of escalating violence, chaos and feeling helplessly trapped where I wasn't only a prisoner for Mick's amusement but I was a prisoner in my own head. This slowly began to create a false reality of who and what I was. There was no longer time or space for me to come to my own conclusions and act upon what I felt was right for my kids and myself.

It didn't matter where I was or what I was doing. All I knew was, I now was isolated not only from the ones I loved but from myself. Effectively, there was an invisible burka that covered my entire existence - all of who I was and wanted to be. If anyone were to pay attention to me, I would get beat up again. In a strange way, the disguise was protecting me at the same time.

I began to notice that I was now an 'object', something Mick owned and kept in control for his own amusement and ability to show off to others as some kind of prized possession. He was extremely addicted to other people's opinions. How they looked at him was crucial to his significance.

I was now a 'product'. I was something Mick owned and possessed. When you observe how much someone obsesses over an object, they will do anything to get it because when they do they feel significant, more powerful, ... loved. However, everything can get old, break and soon grow out of style. We don't want it anymore. We are now faced with the resentment and burden of the responsibility to keep it. Soon the object gets tossed aside and the collector looks for a fresh new version of the much sought after symbol of significance.

As desperate as I was to use this to my advantage, Mick simply would not let me go. The more I wanted out, the more he wanted the chase. It became increasingly apparent to me that Mick wanted to own me because he secretly felt I had all the power! I began to see that there was something substantial I possessed and I wanted to know more.

I look back on the day when I was driving down a winding secluded road headed towards the school my kids attended, to pick them up. I began to scream and hold the steering wheel in such a way that I wanted to break it in half. The rage and feelings of helplessness would no longer lay dormant within me. "I have to get out of this hellish and dangerous nighmare!" Emotions would sound as voices in my head screaming out "You're SO fucked!". There was nowhere to turn. I honestly believed I was going to be imprisoned by this mad man for the rest of my life.

As hard as I tried, I still could not find the answer or a glimmer of hope. Everywhere my thoughts led … would take me to failure. He was way too crazy, too smart and too determined. I was no match for his cleverness and evil undertakings. It was at that precise moment I decided to take my own life. I felt a desperate urge to run my vehicle off the cliff into the relief and freedom from the life that was taking in so much pain and terror.

A quick reminder of the only thing that mattered most in the world to me flashed within my heart. The angelic image of my beloved children rescued me from my panic. If I could go from the extremes of one moment contemplating putting myself to death and then saving my life all within a second … there must be something greater watching and reminding me I still had a shred of sanity within. I knew there had to be another way.

It was clear to me what I believed in. I promised myself that I would trust in that belief. I had an intimate moment with myself and God, there was nothing Mick could do about it. The intimacy and power of this newly realized relationship was invisible to Mick.

I was empowered with this new insight and began to walk another path within my mind. I felt free for the first time in a way I had never recognized before in all my life. This new discovery began to take unique shape and form as to how I was perceiving my situation. I had a lot of work to do. Yet, this time the focus and energy was going to be on me for myself and not on him. I felt I always needed to be ten steps ahead of Mick simply because of what I feared would happen if I wasn't prepared. It was faith that gave me the courage to realize that this nightmare was indeed one not worth believing in.

Wisdom

CHAPTER 4
My life in a bucket

$\mathcal{T}$he fear soon transformed into a curiosity. The curiosity became an interest. The interest became my driving force. I wanted to know more about the other voice that rescued me on that dark day. I became obsessed with this voice within. As a result of being drawn to a power greater than myself, I began to place an opposing thought into my mind every time I noticed when I was feeling terrified and lonely.

When Mick would get angry or was busy trying to gaslight me, I worked on slowing things down in my head to pay more attention to how my body was feeling in the moment. It wasn't long before I noticed, whenever I felt insane or stupid it was because he was actually lying to me. This in itself took time and became self-evident as I stayed committed to my other voice.

I found this new refuge within my head and heart to be my saving grace despite the beatings. As a refugee needing to escape the participation in Mick's unrestrained outbursts I began the pilgrimage towards a private sanctuary within. Don't get me wrong, I was not going to be any better *(at the time)* at stopping him from throwing his fists at me. His rage behind the beating was whipped up to a frenzy that had too much energy behind it to arrest.

If I focused on the intensity, then it was like I was cooperating with it - in my own mind. It seemed to me that I didn't have as much courage as he had anger at the time. But with practice, I believed I could arrange my thoughts to a place where I would no longer be of assistance to the violence.

As difficult as it may be to admit, I was involving myself in the experience and I had to take the energy in another direction - EVEN IF IT WAS ONLY IN MY HEAD!

On an otherwise ordinary day, I walked into the laundry room and was surprised with a gentle drop of water landing on my face. It took me a moment just to take in what was happening as the second drop fell on me in short succession. The effects of the dripping water were taking a toll on the wood floor and I realized action was needed to avoid permanent damage. Naturally, I placed a bucket underneath the leak to protect the floor until a plumber arrived to fix it.

The drips soon started to accumulate in the bucket. But, it was still light and had plenty of space to take in more. One could hardly notice there was a serious leak at all. However, like the creeping aggregate of abuse, the drips kept adding up. My life, just like the bucket, had all the additive assurance of a problem unsolved. It soon enough became full and then. . . overflowed.

If we think of our personal thoughts as drops that leak from a broken belief we may understand better how they can swell up and become so heavy that you can no longer lift the container. The problems spill everywhere into the lives of those around us. This simple metaphor for my life did not escape my awareness.

My bucket of fear was far too heavy for me to think I could change my mess overnight. I knew for sure that I was capable and willing to fill another new container within myself with more liberating thoughts of peace and hope. This new bucket was going to be filled one single thought at a time. I no longer could escape the weight of my new belief system.

In private, I visualized the time I would be far away from all of this kind of thinking that got me into this drama. Remember, I was the one who thought the thoughts that allowed me to participate in this brutal experience I was living. My unconscious old beliefs about myself unintentionally filled the bucket of what can only be seen as a cruel version of confused loving. Now, I can drip the consciousness of loving energy my higher voice was offering, into a new open space within my heart, one loving drop at a time. This took faith and courage.

The old way led me to the edge of a cliff with nowhere to go but down.

Although, there were more experiences of turmoil, helplessness and terror, his destructive energy was in fact, slowly losing power over me. When the dust would settle, I was there in the secret gardens of my mind, planting the delicate seeds of thought which would eventually grow into the enchanted forest of my freedom.

Humility

CHAPTER 5
A victim demands violence

*I*f we find ourselves on the receiving end of harsh words or a fist to the face, you are now consciously or unconsciously participating in the violence itself. Your intention may very well be the complete opposite of this act, yet you can't help but wonder...

How did I get here?

Why is this happening to me!?

This shit happens to other people, not me...

If the violence continues long enough your thoughts turn to 'here we go again...' How do we get from a place of surprise to a place of expectancy?

Why do we allow it to go that far?

Do we want to experience abuse?

Do we feel we somehow deserve the abuse?

Unconsciously, we believe in the violence. Some of us have been witnessing abuse our entire lives. Becoming accustomed to crazy making makes it seem normal. To live any other way, ironically feels unnatural, perhaps even a bit uncomfortable.

Whether we are aware of it or not, we instinctively build walls of protection around ourselves. There, within all of us rests a deeper knowing, like a pearl of wisdom - inviolable. It breathes the truth of our divine nature to find ways to remain safe. We toughen the exterior through our speech, the way we dress, even the way we carry ourselves can be the armor we choose for protection against the predators in our lives.

But who is the villain and where did he or she come from?
The world can be a daunting, dark and violent place. How can we even remotely stay safe in such a reality? For those of us who have been born and raised in the most devastating and hellish of environments, it seems only natural and correct to reflexively protect ourselves and the ones we love from harm. On the other hand, it's incomprehensible to those of us that have not been exposed to such horror.

Who is teaching us this technique for survival and release? Where does all the brutality come from anyway? The cruelty that we inflict on each other is nothing more and nothing less than a ferocious and inarticulate cry for help. When two people in the violent dance were exposed to the same abuse growing up, it might be more natural to expect the same spectacle re-enacted in their own lives as an echo of the past.

WE HAVE LOST OUR MINDS AND WE DON'T EVEN KNOW IT!

We write music with lyrics and harmony to get our point across to those that are willing to listen. We paint and draw images that speak to the eyes that recognize the pain so others can decide to choose rage or compassion. We are dying to share our universal suffering so we don't feel completely isolated and alone within the madness.

We have imprisoned ourselves into believing that pain and suffering are the only choices we have to live by. There is a deep intimacy when people come together in common pain because they can't help but recognize something that feels real and relatable. We look to each other over and over again to fix the broken and missing parts of our happiness and insist that it's our partner that holds the ever elusive missing pieces.

This type of relationship carries within it a promise of inevitable folly, frustration and disappointment. The simple fact remains, everything we project onto others is the reflection of ourselves - not the other person.

We can forever strive to be the person we want others to see, but this is not entirely possible. We can only be the person we choose to see in others. With this in mind, I have come to realize those that act in suffering and violence are the ones carrying the pain they inflict onto others. This is a false sense of empowerment in attempting to control, by way of portraying the role with actions of strength and domination over the one receiving the abuse.

It is now up to the suffering whether they accept the illusion as a bargain. Is it only the oppressed and wounded, that are truly terrified? My suggestion is that perhaps we suffer the misconception of who really has the power in the situation. We tend to lose sight of reality when we become disconnected from what is true.

It all comes down to fear.

At the end of the day, when we take fear for granted it is only as permanent as shadows passing by on the wall. To give up our power for the sake of another human being when they themselves are disconnected from the source, is the stuff of tragedy. We never insist or threaten another unless we believe them to have ownership of something we want. It's the ultimate self-defeat to manipulate ourselves into the belief that it is the other persons fault.

Feeling Abandoned

CHAPTER 6
The irony of peace

*Y*es, I recall the memory when I felt desperate enough to make a stand against Mick. It was still early in the day, however, I was already exhausted from the threats and physical abuse of that particular morning. My four children were all safely away in school at the time, so I felt a surge of personal courage as a call to action. It was comforting to know the kids were distanced from immediate physical harm.

My legs felt weak and unstable, yet I was determined to run out into the driveway and jump into the car to make my escape. The moment Mick got distracted I took the opportunity to run outside and put my desperate and foolish plan into motion. Unfortunately, the driveway was too long for me to outrun Mick's adrenalin fueled sprint as he gave chase like a predator closing in on his prey.

He came up so fast on me - I couldn't even lock all my car doors to keep him out!

Damn it!

Everything was surreal in that it was happening so quickly and so slowly at the same time. I will admit there was a part of me that was still afraid to make my escape in fear of what would happen next. Mick's litany of threats rang like an alarm going off in my head as my hands shook out of control. I felt as if my entire body was in the way. It was like trying to run underwater. I could see myself moving in slow motion as my physical body seemed too feeble to rise to the occasion exactly when it most required precise and instantaneous action to make a break for it!

Mick managed to jump into the back seat of the moving vehicle and take hold of my right arm. He then proceeded to twist and pull with all his might as I lost control of the car. His teeth pressed together as his black eyes spoke of the punishment I was about to receive. I remember looking out to my right just past Mick and I saw several men working in our yard.

Thank God!

Maybe I stand a chance. I can scream for help. As I begged for assistance through the panic and volume in my voice, I was horrified to realize no one would dare to even look at me – let alone come to my rescue. I couldn't believe what I was witnessing. It was now painfully evident as to what was going on. Here I was, a helpless woman being violently attacked and no one was going to help!!!

We wonder why most women don't speak up when they desperately need to cry out for safety. My body began to disconnect from all that I once knew to be real. I was transported into a surreal moment and very much alone.

Am I insane? Do they not hear me? How can they approve of what is happening? I was now a hostage. I was my own witness to the passive agency of others who could not or would not interfere with this drama. Sinking deeper into myself, I could sense Mick feeding off of their supreme discomfort as he took their lack of intervention as a sign of his power ascending in the moment.

Toppling out of the car I stumbled into the house to endure my consequences. I am totally defeated here. Something in the back of my mind knew I had to exhaust Mick of his rage before my kids got home from school. So, I laid there like a good girl and took the totality of the beating. When the brutality got too extreme, I would feel numb for days and sometimes weeks after. As the beatings became more frequent I became disconnected from my body all together.

We each have our own unique way of participating in the insanity of violence.

Some would say these men abandoned me yet I can't help but to realize they were deeply afraid in their own way. When I look back on the men who did nothing to help me, I discovered an insight about them as participants. My heart reminds me that these men had obligation to take care of their own families. Mick was their employer and he was the one that had the power to feed their children. Maybe they acted the same way in their own homes and thought this was normal.

I can only speculate.

Now I choose to thank the experience for showing me that violence hides behind the silence. This was instrumental for me to find the courage and clarity within the experience to make the decision when the time finally came to testify against Mick.

When the time arrived and the choice was staring me in the face I knew I couldn't live like that anymore. It would have been my dubious contribution to all humanity to instigate and prop up abuse if I chose to remain silent.

Empathy

CHAPTER 7

Don't worry. I'll fix you! I'll save you! I'll change you!
(your Goddess has arrived)

*W*hat a fool I was.

"I don't care about the countless warnings or what others have to say about you *(my dear)* because I have a mind of my own damn it - and nothing will stop me from making this relationship work.

I'm a good person.

I am a forgiving person.

I am a compassionate person... Gosh Darn it!

Things will be different now because your true love has finally arrived (ME)! I will not judge you or abandon you. I will always be here no matter what because I'm one of the 'good ones'! '

Whomp-whomp!

Can't tell ya how many times that frame of thought has screwed up my life! If you're going to be one of the 'good guys' then without a doubt, you will need to call in a 'bad guy'. The lines get crossed and the boundaries soon dissolve. Your freedom and sense of peace diminish into a fantasy that can not reach the end unless it ends badly. If we believe we are such good people and we have something others need then the universe will give us the exact partner that fits our expectations. We become unconscious of the fact that we have set up the experience, *(with good intentions of course)* but nonetheless, we set this game up ourselves. Some would call this "co-dependency".

In my experience, there has not been one relationship when I have chosen in an unconscious fashion that has ever failed to pull me into the abyss of hell.

Wait a minute!?!
This was not supposed to turn out this way. I am the master of love and my love should be the very thing that changes your behavior! What went wrong? Wait a minute here - I'm the one who rescues, protects and fixes other people's pain. Why didn't this work out? Why aren't you changing and loving me the way I want you to? Why are you always so dissatisfied with me? I'm doing everything you ask and yet we are both so damn miserable.

If I succeeded in changing, then neither of us could any longer be the same people we were when we first entered into the relationship. Perhaps when the tide turns, we become the one that needs to be rescued. Isn't it strange that the same person who inflicts the pain onto us is the one we expect to rescue us? Do you see the insanity of this? We are both creating absurdity together. It's likeheads or tails on the same coin, no matter how you flip it - we both lose. I soon realized that I was beaten up and abused for the sake of easing his pain and anxiety.

In a frightening way, *(get ready to cringe)* that was what I initially signed up for. Of course, I didn't see the emotional and physical abuse as my intentional way of assisting or saving him. However, that is eventually how it finally manifested When someone is willing to suffer so much for us and us for them, it gives a false sense of significance and love. The tears and repeated promises, "it will never happen again" became a sad, tired and repeated mantra.

Mick's rage howled that it was my fault - his dark idea of what love was caused him to lose his way completely. This eventually led him to an uncontrolled act of fury striking my face and body - - all because he loved me SO much!

The situation went from it being my fault, to his fault, back to my fault and so on like a center court finals match at Wimbledon! Does that sound healthy and loving to you? The score is now LOVE-LOVE or otherwise known as 'zero to zero'. What a crazy making game this is! This played into both the roles of the predator in him and the prey in me. This is a hard pill to swallow because, we don't ever want to give permission for people to act in violence - ever! After all I've been through, I feel compelled to speak my truth about this path and the thought process and misguided beliefs that got me into this dilemma.

These lessons are the ones that eventually set me free.

I could not ignore the new authentic voice that continued to mentor me with clarity and wisdom. Now, I was beginning to understand that the relationship was exactly as promised, even if we both were not aware of it. With recognition, I no longer could continue to believe in the madness - yet the momentum was massive. The Julie that I brought into the relationship was in desperate need to heal. How could I expect things to change if I wasn't willing to do the changing myself?

How am I going to do that?

I literally had no idea how I was going to approach this process, nor was I able to reach out to others without consequence from my tormentor. It seemed I had no one, so I turned inward in search of this new voice once again. She was now my only companion and most trusted friend. The best part was that Mick could not be anywhere near our conversations and that kept me safe ... for the moment.

The energy was slowly shifting.

There was nothing Mick could do or say about it because he could not hear my inner thoughts or even understand how I was feeling. This revelation of my secret inner life was powerful beyond anything the naked eye could see My attention and commitment was tilting towards my authentic voice and not towards him anymore. He would do his dance of violence with me as his partner in this twisted choreography many times again before he would sense something was changing between us.

Mick unconsciously continued to fulfill the secret promise of serving in the role of villain. I chose to focus my energy towards the things that brought me to a place that felt lighter, even if it was just listening to a song that lit me up for a brief 3 minutes. It became evident that if real change were to happen for me, I could no longer focus my attention on the old ways of reacting. Consenting to play the same unconscious role of willing victim was coming to an end.

The old personality I once came in with was soon disappearing regardless of the promise of his. This wasn't always an easy thing to do. In fact, there were many episodes of adrenaline and terror that overwhelmed my ability to focus.

These fierce installments were slowly taking on a new and different meaning for me. I continued to seek refuge in the divine sacred space within the privacy of my own heart. Sometimes just knowing this secret garden was there gave me comfort and hope in a way that I needed to get through yet another painful trial by brute force.

I found myself daydreaming of the kind of life I wanted to be living and noticed how happy I felt in the dream. It occurred to me that I wanted to be with my authentic voice within as much as I could. She was now my very best friend. It was genuinely satisfying to know that I could be intimate and honest with her and not suffer the usual consequences of Mick's unrestrained jealousy. Learning to rely on her and trust in her voice even when I didn't always understand or make sense of her - was becoming essential.

She never once lied to me or misdirected me.

This new orientation became liberating in a way I cannot describe in words alone. Because I was paying attention, it was inevitable that I began to go deeper into the intimacy of this experience more than ever before. Mick couldn't take her away like he did all my other friends or even threaten her life because I was the only one with the permission to access this spirit within myself.

It was around this same time Mick introduced me to Julie. She was the only person he approved of for me to spend time with because she was the wife of his business partner. We both got such a kick out of having the same first name because we were opposite in so many ways, from hair color and taste in clothing–everything!

Mick had effectively eliminated anyone he felt threatened by. This meant he ended up eliminating literally everyone that mattered to me. The jealousy ran so deep, that if he found out I was even talking to a friend, then I could come to expect bruised ribs or a black eye for my trouble.

The need to control and possess me meant he had no problem invading my purse. In order to satisfy his obsession, he helped himself to my cell phone to see who was on my call list. He was incrementally taking any space of mine there was left – he had to fill it in. It became so bad that I started to avoid my phone and therefore talking to people altogether.

It just wasn't worth the abuse.

Mick's spiral of obsession and control over my life, cut everyone out but Julie, who was the only friend I felt I had left. There was no shaking him off of me. Mick even came to my karate classes with Julie who as a bad ass fifth degree black-belt co-owned a martial arts studio with her husband. Was it to keep an eye on me - or was it to make sure he had the same skills I did when it came to self-defense?

I think it was obvious to other people Mick was obsessed with me, but the dirty little secret of the physical abuse was always under the surface. Is it possible she knew intuitively to invite me to a girls only kind of outing? Julie must have sensed the need I had for a kind of escape from the constant hovering of Mick's helicopter surveillance. Fatefully, she landed upon the very thing that would change my life.

Julie chirped, "You are going to love yoga!"

At this point I would have said yes to anything to get some time away. If she had said, "... Want to go with me to the junk yard?" I would have been delighted no matter what the proposition.

"Here, you will need this,", she announced as she handed me my very first yoga mat. In class when someone would call for "Julie, Julie, ... JULIE", they would have to make clear which Julie they were asking for. Since, I had a red mat I became known as Red Julie and my girlfriend was Blue Julie since her mat was the Crayola color of saturated Dodger blue.

While sitting around waiting for class to begin - in walks the instructor, Anya. She reminded me of a gazelle. Her angelic physique was lithe and lean with long arms and even longer legs. Her innocent eyes dominated a beautiful face and expressed a radiant confidence in her yoga body. She entered the studio with such elegance and refinement that I don't think her feet ever touched the ground. This teacher was soft, yet strong and I don't think I ever noticed anyone else before in my entire life exuding both of these qualities at the same time. It was the living embodiment of power and grace.

I wanted to be just like her.
Excuse me, I'll have what she is having!

I was super excited to get started, I couldn't imagine what a beautiful Goddess like her sounded like let alone what she might say.

"Lay on your backs into savasana and notice your breathing" she said.

My head then popped up with a surprised, "Wait – what!?"

"Bring your awareness into your body and observe" she continued.

"What in the hell is she talking about?"

Does she not know that every part of my body aches and throbs not to mention trembles? I was under the impression that I was going to get a vigorous work out so I could tame the fear and anger that I brought into the studio with me. I'm here to get away from my tortured body. I can't even take in a single breath without feeling the grips of anxiety. I had grown accustomed to carrying all of this inside my chest. Christ! I was here to get away from being in any communion with myself!

It hurt to be me.

I knew then and there this was going to be a completely different experience to say the very least. I was willing to see it through after all, anything was better than going home and dealing with the terror that awaited me there. The fact that I was able to get out of the house without Mick latched onto me was a miracle in itself.

I decided to run with it!

"Inhale . . .

Arms overhead . . .

Exhale. . .

Forward fold . . . Step back into downward facing dog . . .

"Holy SHIT!

After Charlie passed I found solace in weight training to focus my energy as an outlet for my aggression for a couple of years. This down dog stuff put all that to shame. I couldn't believe how difficult this pose was. So, you can only imagine my surprise when I learned that this was considered to be one of the resting poses! WTF! We soon began to flow and create forms and shapes with our bodies, all the while mindful of a rhythmic, soothing, breathing technique.
The only focus I remember was on Blue Julie so I could see her body take the shape of the pose and mirror *(as best I could)* to do what she was doing. Other than that, there was a lot to take in, I had only myself to be with for a whole 90 minutes!

Imagine that!

"Lay down onto your backs . . .
Close your eyes and relax your breath . . . Let stillness surround you as you rest and restore your bodies."

Rest and restore your bodies?

I don't know if I can do that. That is precisely the kind of letting my guard down that can get me killed - so I'm not too sure if that is a very good idea. I disecretly peeked one eye open to see if everyone else was buying into this risky suggestion. To my surprise, everyone was indeed lying still as a corpse. Not one peep, not even a sound was heard over the voice of our angelic instructor singing mantras of peace and love.

When Anya was done singing one man had taken it to the next level and fell asleep as he snored through the next five minutes of class! I called upon whatever courage I had and found inside a willingness to surrender to this new teaching. A kind of buzzing sensation in my entire body began to captivate my attention. For the first time in my 36 years of life I felt a gentle silence of genuine compassion resting itself upon me.

We were soon gently brought back to our physical senses again. It was at that precious and powerful moment that I heard the authentic voice inside ...
"We are SO doing this again!"

The only difference this time, was the inner voice seemed to be a little bit closer and a bit louder than ever before.

Giving Voice

CHAPTER 8

If we keep the silence...we protect the violence

I look back on all the years being trapped in a violent home. One thing that stands out in my thoughts is the fact that everything was such a damn secret! I always worried about my kids knowing or seeing too much because they might tell one of their friends or even my parents - and then what!?! The fear of anyone knowing about our dirty little secret terrified me because I knew it would lead to even more violence and maybe one day my death.

Convinced people would not like us anymore or let their kids play with my kids, caused me shame. To even think that I am a crazy woman or troublemaker was a serious threat to my self-esteem. The idea of not being believed was a huge deterrent and could lead to increased wrong doing and humiliation, not to mention further isolation. Mick had a way with people. He was very good at getting others to need him and think he was a great guy. He loved to get into people's deepest insecurities and convince them that he held the golden ticket so they could get what they so desperately needed. Money was the most significant influence for Mick. Most people see that as the only way to solve many of their problems.

When I now speak to groups of people on behalf of all survivors of domestic violence, the most persistant reactions I hear are:

"Why didn't you leave?"

"How come you didn't tell anyone"?

"You don't look like a woman that would be a victim - let alone allow someone to abuse you."

These are very valid questions and commonly asked with good reason. When we think of women in abusive homes we tend to resort to the image of certain races, cultures, and even an economic status that we think of as typical. The fallacy is, we allow ourselves to wrongly think others just live a life immune to this violence somehow. This isn't how things are, unfortunately. To understand the answers to these questions we need to open our hearts and create a safe place for the women to answer them without violent and terrifying consequences.

The truth shall set you free, ... really? How about the truth will get your ass kicked or possibly tortured and killed!

Yup, that's a lot more like it. If this is what happens to the terrified women who want the violence to end so desperately - the silence seems to be the safest solution.

The violence will always hide in the shadows of secrets... always. What is a woman or child to do when they feel there is nowhere to turn? Many women report domestic and sexual abuse only to find we have inherited a system where traditionally the power structure is painfully tilted towards the accused. Ironically, the perpetrator has long since seemed to have a stronger support system built in to protect his legal rights.

Violence always breeds more violence...

What can a woman do? Where can she go to receive the help she desperately needs for herself and her children so they can be safe? There has been a stigma on women in violent homes.

Unfortunately, there still exists an outdated attitude coming from uneducated law enforcement officers that focuses more upon correcting the women instead of prosecuting the men. If the woman becomes more resigned because of this *(and how could she not?)* the perpetrator is empowered by both the lack of consequence and her essential diminishment.

Stuff that cops say . . .

"There is really nothing we can do, Mam." *(our hands are tied here).*

"Why don't you just pack up and leave so he can calm down?" *(and I can get back to my patrol car).*

"What did you do to provoke him so he felt he needed to hit you"? *(she must love it).*

It is not unusual to hear this kind of hard-boiled judgement coming from a peace officer responding to women's reluctant and panicked phone calls. Any naïve hope they may have had for justice can be crushed in one fell swoop. We as human beings can get numb to things. The victim gets numb to survive the beatings. The police officer may become desensitized to the trauma on the job, sometimes out of a sense of self-preservation.

The question remains, where can a woman turn to for help if she can't even be safe when she calls the police? Her only hope is to keep her mouth shut and live her life on pins and needles. The delicate dance around her partner is always in the hope that today's performance won't be the day that she or her children end up on the receiving end of a discreetly broken bone or worse - lose their lives!
How do we find the courage to break the silence and know that we will be safe? This question rang through my head every single day for more than four years. I honestly believed that I was stuck and had nowhere to go. Yet, I could not accept that this was actually happening! I would look back and obsess on all the things I would have or could have changed, like . . . not showing up for dinner the night I met Mick.

Jesus!

The bullshit excuses Mick would give to explain and defend his behavior away seem unbelievable to me now. He would tell me that I needed to be forgiving. Then, he would lay it on thick about how special I was to be loved so much. How could I possibly leave him when he needed me? What kind of a woman would do such a thing like, abandon the man that loves her?

Mick would go as far as to lock me in a closet overnight after a beating and explain to our guests *(and my children)* the next morning that I wasn't feeling well or I simply didn't want to get out of bed. The more insane he became, Mick would be sure to let others believe I was the one with the problem. I was the bitch being so difficult, indifferent and rude.

There were times when he would convince my children that I simply didn't care. He brazenly claimed that I suffered from depression. Mick had my incapacitation to back up his deception. He used it to full effect. This helped create doubt. In taking advantage of the sharing of false information Mick knowingly fostered the direct intention of damaging my relationships.

He wanted to sever things between my kids and me.

Just as he had done with everyone else in my life, he deliberately ran interference between Mother and child whenever the opportunity arose. If one of my kids came to knock on our bedroom door and wanted to snuggle with mom he would intercept and send them away with a declaration to the tune of, "She doesn't want to see you now!" This simple cruelty created serious long term problems down the line with me and my little ones.

There was a helpless feeling that overtook the silence.

It grew so big that I didn't even know if I had the strength to fight all the bullshit Mick presented to my family and friends. It's just too all encompassing! I was alone without friends and support. I soon began to question my own ability to make decisions and do things right without getting into trouble with Mick. Eventually, I was losing sight of what was real and what was manipulation.

Up to this point, I had to maintain the image of a happy and lucky woman to keep Mick from getting mad at me. I remember how my heart would sink and heat would trail down my body when he would start to rage. It felt like my spirit would die a little bit more every time he would get bent out of shape. There came a time when he would threaten my friends and even their children. No one was safe there anymore and I had no one to go to for reassurance of my sanity that was slipping away from me. The beatings became more severe and far more frequent.

The scenes I look back on seem so insane and unrealistic to me today. The idea of one person being so cruel and reckless with another - rattles my soul. I found myself doing and saying anything I needed to do to keep him pacified. But as time moved forward, nothing I did or could do made him happy. He would find any reason he needed to beat me and berate my children.

Mick raged that I wasn't doing all I could to make the relationship work.

One famous fit of jealousy opened with Mick in a moving car. He had a set of needle nose pliers pressing the points with significant force into my ribs. Mick was using the threat of imminent puncture wounds as the alternative to his demands that I open the door and jump out. The option was to jump or to be repeatedly stabbed as I sat there too terrified to exit the car at high speed.
Shit happened so fast - I was completely stunned.

He reached over grabbing the back of my head by my scalp and smashed my face into the dash board while steering the car with his other hand. In the middle of all this, it became more clear he was triggered over a colleague of ours who dared to show concern for my well-being. While making a delivery to our home she had inadvertently witnessed him killing rabbits with a pellet gun in the back yard of our house simply because they had eaten his flowers.

He would shoot them without remorse.

As they were hit, they would cry out in animal pain. Before Mick's horrible act, I didn't even know bunnies could make this sound. He would dispose of their dead bodies in the trash can. The more this provoked my friend (who was clearly an animal lover) the more perverse pleasure he seemed to take in her anguish. As a colleague and my friend knew something few others did. She knew he was not the hero he pretended to be to the outside world. She had his number and a voice of her own. Anyone who dared to challenge him like that - set him off.

The attack stopped only when he pulled our car abruptly into a public car lot and left me alone while he walked far enough away that I wouldn't hear the call. On that call he issued a death threat to my friend.

It was all my fault...

In some crazy way, I felt responsible for putting my friend in harm's way. If she didn't care about me she wouldn't be the focus of his rage. I would rather him just hit me than to turn his furor to people I love. He was in a complete raving frenzy at this point. After hours of this random, impulsive and meandering road show, we arrived home. Mick's bottomless pit of malcontent bile boiled over inside the car while sitting in the driveway. He continued this 'how dare you!?" version of body punishment.

I knew Mick was starting a new tantrum when he turned the car stereo way up high to mask his verbal attacks. It turns out there was method to his paranoid madness. It only served to double the intensity of it all because he was so in my face. Mick had to scream at the top of his lungs to make himself heard over the pulsing techno music.

"I know you have a tape recorder in your purse!" he accused.

This showed not only was he out of his mind, but he was afraid of exposure and people finding out. More than that he doubled down on the physical intimidation if I had any notion of leaving. His attack of choice at this point in this fevered pitch was to go straight for the jugular. Mick reveled in delivering devastating body blows, and the slamming my head up against anything solid that stood behind me.

The cruel calculation of inflicting heaps of agony and damage without actually hospitalizing me was always in the measure of how much to dish out in his ritual attacks. I remember his hand wrapped around my throat after several punches to the gut as if this was the natural follow up. This ritual included a sadistic game where he savored my inability to catch a breath. While he sat on my chest with his knees pinning my shoulders down so he had full control over my body and how much life I could breathe into it at any time.

Eventually I got out of the car. I don't remember how - It was all a blur to me at this point - but I managed to get into the house. At the time, the Lake Sherwood country club house we lived in was 9,000 square feet large with two grand staircases. Sheepishly, I tipped-toed up the smaller back staircase in hopes of my kids not getting a glimpse of me in my current condition. The thought of running into them was unbearable - I had to avoid being seen like this.

Somehow or another I managed to sneak my way down the hall and into my private master bathroom. Quick as I could, I locked the door behind me and turned on the shower. Desperate and exhausted, I stepped my dilapidated body under the warm streaming water. Closing my eyes, I could feel the comfort but also the sting of washing the filth off from my face. My time alone was cut short as Mick managed to unlock the door skulking in with a camera in his hand. Flashes of light blinded me as I stepped away in a panic. I screamed, begging him to stop. Covering up my private parts with my hands and arms was a pitifully inadequate shield to keep me from further violation. Micks hand grabbed my throat once again.

"Put your fucking hands down and sit still - or I'll squeeze harder."

Mick wasn't finished with me yet. He made a choice to sexually violate me for the first time on that horrible day.

Divinity Within

CHAPTER 9

Do you want to die in violence, or die in peace?

$\mathcal{I}$ just got my ass kicked and all I could think about were the glorious moments of refuge on the yoga mat in the studio. I continued to open the windows in my heart. After the healing of my body, I was taking several classes a week *(with Mick's permission of course)*. Diving into the deep end of this spiritual practice I was an absolute beginner. I couldn't get enough of this experience in chanting and meditation. This was a revelation I simply could not get enough of!

Yum-yum ...YUM!...

On the surface, my yoga time did not appear to be any threat to Mick. He considered the whole business of yoga to be a joke anyway. Once in a while he would come to class to try it - but it was too hard for him. The main thrust of the practice was to place the focus upon oneself. This was not his idea of a good time. His place of power was more in the realm of making money and controlling others, not spending time in deep self-reflection.

Even in yoga I was super competitive with myself. Suffering the beginners mind, I noticed my ego was seeking a kind of perfection which was messing me up. I was trying too hard. The practice is a balance of softening and breathing. The truth is, I was grateful for the escape because the more I learned - the more I wanted to learn. I had discovered a place of peace. This is when I realized my internal work with yoga is connected to my purpose *(Dharma)* in life.

Shift happens.

As a life-long habitual fixer of other people, I can remember wishing how much I wanted Mick to discover something like this to throw himself into. No matter what I did - it didn't seem to change what he was doing. Spiritually, I was creating a new direction for myself.

Glimpse after glimpse.

I started to see almost everything in a new way.

Who am I?

What made me think I knew anything at all?

How can I fix anyone else if I myself am so confused?

What business is it of mine to think anyone else needs to be fixed by me.

Last time I asked God ... he let me know he didn't need my help today.

Previously, the little girl in me had actually wanted Mick to rescue me so I wouldn't have to do the work. Now, at long last, I was finally responsible for my own mind, body and spirit.

My children relied on me to find my sanity for the sake of their survival and sense of security. There wasn't much of that left by this time, yet, I was determined to try something different so we could escape the insanity we were all living in. As I steadily continued to practice on my yoga mat, I took the wisdom with me throughout the days. Lectures from Paramahansa Yogananda became a ritual of daily reading as I continued to strengthen the relationship with myself. The "other voice" came closer and closer as I began to notice and feel her presence.

This new voice.

My authentic voice.

Deep down it was always there.

Now it remains, but only just barely under the surface - closer to me than my own skin.

This relationship with myself was growing stronger. The profound love I felt for the divine within me was overriding anything and everything negative that surrounded me. My thoughts were saturated with all the things that made me feel miraculous. The farther I traveled along on this path of illumination, the more impossible it became to go back to the way things were with Mick.

The more time passed in this state of mind - the further away Mick felt to me.
He would remain unchanged from the man I met and initially fell in love with. Mick was becoming unrecognizable to me and me to him - because I was changing and he wasn't. It was still frightening at times, yet I couldn't help but to notice he

was becoming a bit intimidated by my lack of victim like response that once was so thrilling to him.

I began to see how ridiculous his stories were and how frightened HE actually was as he tried to bulldoze me with his towering rages.

"Just give me a reason to hit you!" He would bark.

(Act of Violence) Two people acting in violence...

Soothing myself included seeing how this guy was the victim. Mick was indeed the one who was most terrified. No longer intimidated by this man's manipulations, I chose not to participate in the same old way. My conscious awareness was changing. This was no longer an unconscious dance between partners.

Because of this change, I could no longer play the same tired part or read from the same brutal script. It was time to let go of my playing the powerless victim to his powerful villain in this redundant attack scene. When I didn't give Mick the sick satisfaction of my cowering in fear of his power, the intensity of his grip would weaken through disappointment. It wasn't as much fun for Mick anymore.

At the peak of the financial crisis of 2007-2008, we sold the Sherwood home and took up in another of the three homes we owned. The largest of which was in Mureau Estates. This house was my favorite of all we owned. In the design tradition of a Tuscan villa the place even came dedicated with a plaque in Italian reading, *il Mio Tramonto*, which roughly translates to My Private Sunset. There were only ten other estates in this exclusive private gated community.

We lived in the house on the top of the hill. It was a sprawling 5,500 square foot single story with two separate garages on each end of the house to contain the five to six cars we would have. At any given time, Range Rover, Porsche 911 *(cabriolet)*, Escalade, Mercedes CL550 and BMW M3's decorated our driveway as a matter of reflecting our external status symbols.

Inside the estate were more than a dozen chandeliers. Having had a hand in designing the whole place, my walk in closet showcased it's vaulted ceilings with yet another chandelier. Cascading a shimmering light on all of the spacious shelves one could see a panorama of designer shoes and iconic purses – all the latest collections.
What girl wouldn't want this fantasy fit for a princess?

Unfortunately for me, it was also the dead end of a crime scene for my violent partner to get away with beating, strangling and threatening me on a regular basis.

How many times was I sure I wasn't going to get out of this elegant yet deadly space alive? Mick locked me inside all night on occasion to serve his conviction that I had indeed 'learned my lesson' if I had dared to displease him. In hindsight, my luxurious personal space within the closet was, in fact, a perfect location for secret and sadistic mayhem. No matter how loud I tried to scream my misery would be muffled by this sound-proof chamber.

I hated that closet and everything in it.

How could I not resent the beautiful things that filled it? It was standard practice for Mick to present the gift of a new designer purse or an elegant pair of shoes after a severe beating. It was as if, I earned it, because he was entertained by my pain. It was evident that he felt a need to not only relieve himself of the guilt but moreover, cleaned the slate so to speak, to free up his karma bank account for another beating.

He thought he was the master of deception.

Others would notice and comment on the new, beautiful and obviously expensive gifts. The illusion it created was of a thoughtful and generous man who adored his partner. Mick was the greatest guy ever! Which in turn, made me look like the luckiest girl ever - right? The big homes, fancy gifts, the diamond rings and flashy cars were just part of a calculated campaign of overt propaganda to keep his dirty, violent secrets hidden from the world.

Putting on a fake smile to not give the secret away made me feel phony.

Mick relished in dictating how I would wear his latest gifts. He would humiliate me in front of people by running down how very expensive they were and how great he was, to buy me all these things.

Glorified violence.

The secret was sealed in the paradox between how beautiful these decoys were as ornaments and the suffering they symbolized to me personally. It was normal for Mick to brag about his wealth and love for me. He would comment continuously about how the diamond rings he gave me were a reflection on him and how lucky in fact, I was to be his girl. This self-aggrandizing tactic continued until the authentic Julie I was growing into became awakened to the reality of what was happening and what my part was in the story.

Fortunately, I was able to spend time with Blue Julie because her husband worked with Mick. The four of us would often go out to dinner together. I began to feel I could confide in her. But, the more time we spent together, the less and less Mick was able to contain his rage and intention to control me even though it would make a scene right in front of our friends. It was slowly, yet surely coming to pass that my authentic self was in the inextricable process of pulling away. In my mind, all I believed about Mick and his insane behavior was changing, forever.

I learned you don't want people coming near you because it can only mean trouble.

Now, I had the support from a respected and trusted friend. I felt validated. I was not crazy nor making a big deal out of nothing. Those of us that have been in extremely abusive environments for an extended period of time tend to get our boundaries completely distorted.

What did I do wrong and how can I fix it?

Perhaps he is right and I deserved it.

It's really not that bad … it could have been worse *(downplaying it)*.
If only I had listened and understood better - I would not have upset him!

My old thoughts describe in perfect detail the absence of any self-esteem.

All these false accusations I had placed on myself were slowly dissolving away. I thanked my voice of wisdom for bringing light into the darkness of my life *(little by little)* as I started to notice what was really happening here. I was no longer choosing to believe in this terrifying narrative. My life story was no longer determined by this partner and his fiction.

My self-realization developed, *(glimpse by glimpse)* through meditation and self-reflection. The books I read were captivating my imagination and gently brought more clarity into my consciousness. I discovered a truth about myself and it was liberating. Once, I tasted this nectar, I couldn't get enough of it! My reactions were shifting and my visions of freedom intensified. My gut instincts were reconfiguring and becoming more apparent. My part in the powerful play with Mick turned away from the melodrama and looked straight into the horizon of the opposite direction.

The transfer of energy was shifting with great power and velocity. My private thoughts included moments of peace, feelings of love and glimpses of joy - even while in the surroundings of chaos. I couldn't help but notice the confusion in Mick as he realized I was pulling away. It was as if we could no longer identify one another. I wasn't the same wounded dove Mick met several years ago. But now, he was no longer a man I could recognize as a lover, a partner or even my friend.

Having taken a giant step back, I was no longer willing to be his prize or property to abuse and control. The beatings continued like a broken down familiar routine. However, the energy building up in me was not subsiding and that was the one thing he had absolutely no control over! I found it impossible after eight months of self-discovery to abide by the story we had written together for so many years. My heart changed and therefore my life had to follow. Some way, somehow, I had faith that release was right there waiting for me with its arms wide open!

The awareness and strength I was accumulating inside could now be seen on the outside. My future prospects were as buoyant as a rising tide. I was more my authentic self now then I *(or anyone else)* had ever known. Even in this expansive mode, I'll admit I still had no idea how I was going to get out of this hostile environment. But I did know good things were going to happen because I was learning to trust the knowingness in my body. The episodes when I thought I was going insane, confused or lost in Mick's behavior were decreasing like footprints on the windblown sand.

It was a Friday evening and the stress and emotions were building up within Mick as he had recently made some bad business deals that were profoundly affecting his revenue stream. Mick was unfamiliar with things not going his way and I could see him slowly delaminating. He was spinning out of control. He wanted us to go out for some cocktails with his friends to let off some steam. Of course, I was very reluctant due to past experiences with Mick's intoxicated episodes leading straight into a violent outburst.

It was exhausting just thinking about the aftermath that would drag into the closet until the early hours of the morning after. Here I was at the fork in the road and did not know what to do next. Then, I prayed to God to help get me through the unknown journey ahead. I had to keep my mind clear from all thoughts that left me in a place of vulnerability. At that exact moment, my phone rang with my pal Blue Julie on the other end asking where we were going to meet.

I looked overhead and said, "Thank you God!"

It was all I could think to say first when she told me she and her hubby were meeting us there because I felt safer with her there.

The evening started out with the civilized veneer of welcoming hugs and even laughter as we began to chat and order our food. The drinks started to pour in and the laughter gained momentum as the evening progressed. Soon, reports of Mick's drunken behavior made its way over to me as one of the wives complained of his inappropriate and sexual advances towards her. It was interesting that it was such a hush-hush thing and no one wanted to make a big deal out of it. Again, I came face to face with the dangerous notion of when people practice keeping secrets to protect the violator and not the one who receives the violation.

The tension was disabling me.

I walked outside to catch a breath of fresh air. How I was going to get home safely? Julie's husband had not participated in the drinking of alcohol that evening, so I felt it best to ask him to drive us home. He was more than happy to do so and invited Mick to come with us to his car. Mick snapped and lost his temper as he hollered out loud, "What a fucking bitch I was and how dare I disrespect him in front of others. You will get your fucking ass in this car right now or I will throw you in myself" he screamed.

To avoid being pitched into the car I announced for all to hear, ...

"Mick, I don't mean any disrespect..
but I don't feel safe with you driving
after you have been drinking, ... "

Oh shit!

His teeth began to grind and his glare was like a sword piercing right through my throat. The crowd soon began to gather around and I caught myself feeding into the lunacy as I surrendered into the car to keep the peace for that moment in time. As he screeched out of the parking lot he would stretch his head out of the window and holler out to his friends, 'look I'm fine and I can drive - stupid bitch doesn't know what she is talking about!'.

Thankfully we made it home without a car crash.

All I wanted to do was get in the house, change my clothes and pray he falls to sleep right away. I made my way into the closet so I could change into my jammies. I consciously spoke only in soothing and kind words to Mick with the intention of calming him down. I thought for an all too brief a moment I was out of the woods - but that all changed in a flash of anger.

Mick abruptly interrupted my ploy to calm him with a dark look right at me. I witnessed his deep brown eyes turn to a black and hollow glare. This has always been one of the tell-tale signs that all hell was about to break loose. The deep dark shadow that covered the windows of his soul told me – woman, get ready for a serious beating.

"FUCK ME!"

It was all I heard as the terror took hold of my inner voice and silenced her. The trembling started to take over and my breath could no longer remember itself. His hand quickly wrapped itself around my throat as he lined up with me face to face. His teeth were clenched and the right corner of his mouth lifted in frustration and rage. Perhaps this was going to be the time he would squeeze the life right out of me.

At times I've been reluctant to fight back at all in fear that it would only escalate the rage and cause me even more harm. But, I had no choice now as the constriction around my throat prevented me from taking another breath.

"You fucking whore! How dare you disrespect me like that, I'm going to fucking kill you and your kids will suffer the consequences. I will have your daughters raped and beaten.
Your boys will never walk again!
You stupid bitch, you don't even know who you are fucking with!"

I instinctively jammed my thumbs up into his armpits in hopes that I could catch a breath as I was slowly losing consciousness. He quickly stepped back in shock that I would do such a thing. Time stood still as we looked straight into each other's eyes without either one of us moving an inch.

In that lingering moment my voice was set free as she so clearly and without hesitation turned the light on in my mind and in my heart. It was the kind of incisiveness only the divine could have offered to me. The grace and strength of truth took me over and opened my eyes to what was really happening. The voice was telling me something new ...

'Mick is terrified.

This does not belong to you.'

I was stunned and could not help but to notice, he was too. Perhaps, I gave off some sort of look or gesture. Maybe the power of something unfamiliar held him without moving - I don't know. Yet, I needed to be with that voice. Because, it was the only one that made any sense to me at the time. There was a booming strength and confidence that carried my voice out into the closet and filled the space with dominion.
"YOU CAN NOT TOUCH ME," I shouted.

"You might be able to kill and even torture my body but MY WILL and PERMISSION will never be granted! YOU CAN NOT HAVE ME. I WILL NOT EXTEND OR GIFT YOU THE SACRED PART OF ME THAT YOU CANNOT TOUCH OR SEE. I AM FREE NO MATTER WHAT YOU CHOOSE TO DO. I BELONG TO JULIE AND JULIE SAYS NO!

That moment everything insane began to reveal itself to me as a lie. I was then given the opportunity to see within his hollow eyes how unloved and lost he believed himself to be. Shut out from the world, abandoned and terrified. He looked so frightened and hopeless. Hopeless enough to kill someone he thought he loved to satisfy his need to feel important and significant.

Somehow, someway he convinced himself into believing I possessed what he needed to survive. All this time, it was me that held the so-called power and he wanted to take it.

Didn't he know that he already had it all along?

The moment of truth soon passed and another wave of rage possessed Mick into throwing me across the closet and choking me once more while pressing his knees onto my chest. I went limp and did not resist. His fists repeatedly pounded my body and face. My hair was pulled as leverage to move me out from the closet just to be dragged back in again. This fight was his and I no longer wanted to be a participant in it even though I was frightened.

I consciously called out to God for a miracle.

In the midst of this shit storm, it occurred to me that if he indeed was going to take my life in the next few moments I could choose for myself to die in his violence or instead die in my peace.

After what seemed like a long drawn out beating even for Mick he began to curl up into the corner of the closet and cry. "Why can't you love me?" He sobbed. I felt a wave of compassion that was not only offered to him but to myself as well. I did not feel sorry for him because I was now looking at the behavior for what it was not what it appeared to be. To offer him my pity no longer made sense to me as it did in the past. The only person I was now left with was myself. I knew that I could not save him or our relationship, nor was there any point to continue this insane illusion of this twisted version of a choked-out love.

Humility took a giant step forward as I recognized the victim I had for so long believed Julie to be. I wanted to shake this realization off, but the truth of my inner authentic voice would not allow it to happen. It was indeed an uncomfortable discovery about myself, yet I knew it was true. I then realized, as long as I continued to support the victim within, I would always be in need of an actor in the supporting role. That was Mick's part in this script and we both played out our characters to the hilt.

I began to see that as long as I was in fear of this man, he would continue to appear as my teacher and tormentor in one form or another. If not him, then another would be sure to appear to grant me that calling. Mick and I were in this together as we continued throughout all those years collaborating in our pain as a dysfunctional couple. I will never forget the moment of divine intervention Mick and I experienced in that closet. Even after all the violence, tears and grief we shared, desperate and unconsciously calling out to be loved - I was released that night.

I had finally broken free from the ignorance that held me hostage for so many years.

At this point that I had to stay close with my divine self and listen as if my life depended on it. My faith continued to strengthen, as the self-deceptions of being a victim could no longer override the truth and carry me further into a dysfunctional hell. The days were now continuing to be filled with thoughts of self-love and compassion rather than the false identity of victim and or villain, even though the physical violence continued albeit with less energy.

It was unsustainable.

We were at the cross-roads of our relationship.

I was no longer going to believe in the fear that had me within its grip before.

The truth is it was never real and didn't have power over me in the first place.

Inner Voice

CHAPTER 10
Secret Oasis

*W*e were falling apart as a couple.

I was no longer the same naïve girl I once was and the ramifications were apparent. The ability to continue to live the way we were was now impossible. We were no longer the same people with the same mindset that kept the storyline of violence alive.

If we don't feed the monster it will be sure to die. This is exactly what was beginning to happen. The drips and drops of insight were filling in me a new consciousness and spilling out into the energy field around me. It's interesting to notice the transition taking place without a single word spoken or gesture made. We both could sense the undeniable shift beneath our feet as if the newfound stability within my secret garden rumbled the bedrock of this relationship's past.

Something big was coming.

I would catch myself whenever he would try to distract me into one of his cagey ploys to keep me entangled in the territory of his choice – a state of fear. The manipulation game would continue as we played our cards back and forth without a clear winner. It wasn't going anywhere. I was still living in the same home with the same man yet the story continued to unravel. He kept doing the same old thing only I was slowly starting to separate myself from this zero-sum game like an endless tic-tac-toe.

Hostage no more.

Emerging like a phoenix from the fire to catch her first breath of freedom from a dark imprisonment, she handed me the insight I had been waiting so long for. I was still aware of the danger I was surrounded by day by day. But the key to willingness opened the lock to see myself within the situation differently. If I continued to focus my energy on the things I believed in and knew to be true for myself what I choose to watch, listen to, and become a part of were all mine to entertain. Mick continued to lose his temper and put his hands on me but the power behind it seemed different. Perhaps we no longer shared residence within the mindset of tyrant and slave any longer. The threats and lies had no place within me to hold sway. At least for now my focus was going to be how to get my kids and myself physically out.

It's critical to have a plan of action pieced together between yourself and your children. If the siren goes off and the opportunity presents itself to get out safely we had to be ready. When you feel danger closing in many terrifying thoughts can easily sink your plan of escape. The opportunity is to be willing to change something about what you believe and whom you really believe in. Yes, he can cause great harm, yet, there is something very compelling and subtle that has the ability to assist you.

Your Higher Self!

This Higher Self knows and sees all even during the times we don't think we are moving beyond what appears to be the obstacle. Looking back, I have come to understand my relationship with myself as Julie. She was the one who had experienced an entire life through the eyes and beliefs of others since she was born. Now with the knowledge of the Higher Self *(that created me in the first place)* I could never see and experience the world in the same way again.

 It is like any other relationship, the more time you spend together and the more experiences you share, the closer you become. Our closest relationships help shape ways of thinking and behavior. Even the ones that caused the most grief and violence become predictable. If we didn't study and get to know the perpetrator we would not have survived this long.

The part of us that once seemed a distant stranger becomes the one we know best after much time spent together. We gently trust in this friend little by little. Once in a while we realize we were not listening. Maybe logic is what distanced ourselves away from her. Yet, there she is, always listening and waiting for us to hear without a single judgment or care of the past. Pure love and unconditional truth is all she knows.

She is patient and kind.

She has no knowledge of the suffering we create for ourselves. How can you be a vibration of love and fear at the same time? You cannot. It is we as our personalities that have the freedom to choose as many times as we wish. There is no one else holding us back from the joyful and healthy lives we cry out for but ourselves. The acknowledgement and truth of this reality was all I needed to be willing to realize myself out of misery and into a life of liberation.

The Warrior

CHAPTER 11
The Shift

June 2008 was the end of yet another negotiated six month extension of our relationship which was Mick's practice in postpoing the inevitable end. The kids would be out of school and we would finally be through our term of staying in this malevolent accord. How many times had Mick begged, bargained or just beat me into submission to keep me in control and buy more time before the terminal end of this impossible alliance. His bargaining chip was brutally simple.

If you leave today - I'll just kill you.

"If you stay for another six months I'll let you go without any harm to you and your kids." Then that time would expire and he would try to reintroduce to another version of the futile extension. It was evident that I was already gone, just not yet physically. It's almost like I agreed to be a prisoner in exchange for the continued safety of my kids.

His thought process was, "You are not going to want to leave me in six months, because I will be such a better person. I swear to GOD."

After the first and second time, I knew he wouldn't keep the promise to let me go. If I gave him what he wanted in the moment, maybe he would stop. Anything to stop the immediate punching, slamming, kicking and beating of my body. I would surrender in the moment. There was a point in time when I believed the only way out was if I was going to kill him or he was going to kill me.

Mick would just laugh. If that were to happen, the possibility of my being jailed would leave my kids without a mom. How could I abandon my children through being imprisoned?

On June 27 th , nearing the end of this term, a surreal feeling of calm came over me and for no particular reason. I joined up with blue Julie to help clean up her karate studio. I remember feeling a strong intuition that the end of the road was coming up fast in my life. When I told Julie of my premonition, somehow I just knew I would be free within the next day or so. I was certain that something extreme was going to come to the fore with Mick and that he was headed for a major freak out for the last time.

The feeling took my breath away.

Blue Julie looked at me with wonder. How could I feel both the terror anticipating the ritual of violence about to be set off and look forward to freedom at the same time? I just knew in my bones it was going to be ugly and I couldn't explain it.

Without a doubt the crucible of the volcano was about to erupt. There was no reasoning or even detail behind this knowing. By this time, I had established a close relationship with my higher voice. Based on experience, I knew it would be useless to ignore my own wisdom. Something within me felt protected and separated from what was about to take place. It's strange, as if I knew exactly what was going to happen and I was observing myself in a way that moved faster and slower than what I was experiencing in real time. Maybe this is the very definition of traumatic distress.

Blue Julie then offered me an enveloping gaze of compassion and clarity, as if she knew too. I will always love her for knowing her own wisdom and sharing it with me. I trusted her with my life and I knew she was my true friend. We shared a moment of concern as she trusted in my words and cared about my safety. It seemed pointless to prepare for the unknown, yet, something mysterious in my higher power wanted me to know all that was necessary to stay alive.

GET READY AND TRUST IN ME was the mantra that continued to speak itself as the day unfolded into the evening.

Mick's behavior was erratic and filled with panic.

There was an awareness of anticipation in the air that neither of us could deny.

It was understood that he was going to release my children and myself in June when the kids got out of school for the summer. I know this sounds all a bit crazy and it was. Everything was out of control and made absolutely no sense about maintaining this way of doing things, but he had to take control any way he felt he could to buy time. I will never understand Mick's thinking on this, except perhaps for his futile attempt at exerting dominance and a sense of power when he feared he was losing control.

The evening grew dark and Mick was out at a bar by himself on the prowl. Apparently there were two women he was stalking. They were not interested in him and this threw Mick into a deeper panic. He called me to pick him up with the excuse that he had been drinking *(as if that ever mattered in the past)*. I showed up to see him sitting next to the two women as he abruptly gabbed my arm to pull me aside and instructed me as to what I was going to tell them *(to sooth his ego)*.

The setting was a typical place to pick up on people, as bars and dance clubs go. What I noticed was that the music was so loud Mick had to shout to be understood which made the conspiring all the more absurd. Mick seemed desperate and panicked to be in this position. He needed my help in creating a cover story to save face from their rejection.

"You need to tell them that you are my wife!!!", he demanded.

I wasn't going to feed into the nonsense by trying to make sense of his request, so I walked over to the women and reluctantly told them that I was his wife with an obvious roll in my eyes that only they could see. There was a clear and subtle understanding that was exchanged as the three of us spoke without words. They smiled at me with concern and left the restaurant. "It was very nice to meet you, ... " they said as they gave me a sympathetic handshake.

"YOU CAN'T LEAVE ME!" He pleaded.

Mick sat at the bar to the left of me. I didn't want to look at him. I could see him in the reflection in the mirror behind the bartender...

"YOU CAN'T LEAVE ME!"

"I promise, I will never hurt you or treat you badly again!"

"I'm begging you Julie, . . . you can't do this to me!"

His despairing, yet hopeful pleas were his last-ditch effort to keep me from escape. There was nothing that he could have said or done at this point to prevent me from leaving - because I had already left in spirit. Mick had no clue as to the mental strength I had built up within myself.

It must have occurred to Mick on some level that I would rather have him kill me, than for me to stay with him again - for any length of time.

A bursting realization took over as a hot flash of fear spiked the natural beating of my heart. I gasped to catch a breath and met with the reality that I was there to drive him home! I was afraid and certain of what he was capable of doing when he was in a desperate panic. I didn't want him anywhere near my children and I needed to quickly come up with a plan to keep us safe.

I had absolutely no ideas, no safe place, no inside voice at this point!

My first move was to stall the situation until something that made sense to me presented itself. My words were the only option I could think of to convince him that everything was going to be ok, so that was what I used. "Mick, let's get some rest so we can talk about this in the morning." I pleaded. I would soften anything and everything that he would say to get him to relax, even if it meant we had to stay at the restaurant all night long. Once I was able to see the pupils in his eyes, I knew I stood a better chance of safety. We eventually made it home and I managed to get some sleep without a beating that night, if only because I stayed up as if my life depended on being awake longer than Mick.

Looking back, it still amazes me that l survived one day at a time for years on end in that life with this man.

Compassion

CHAPTER 12
The morning after

$\mathcal{J}$une 28th, 2008.

7:00am.

The safety of slumber couldn't last forever.

I remember waking up, startled by Mick being literally in my face. He was so close I could feel his hot, rancid breath as he worked himself up into a fury. How long was he sitting there watching me sleep? It's as if he was waiting there as long as he needed to for me to wake up, so he could have the most intimidating effect possible.

His rage was evident as his teeth pressed together and his head began to tremble with the intensity of the coming storm.

"You aren't going anywhere! Do you understand me?"

"You will do as I say and love me the way you were always supposed to - or you will suffer the consequences.

" His rampage would stretch to the threats of killing me, to not killing me. The very idea of keeping me alive to endure the agonizing grief of my children being tortured and murdered, put a smile on his face as he laughed in delight at his own sadistic cleverness.

I knew the moment had arrived and the warning I received the day before had not failed me. Here we go!

DEAR GOD PLEASE DON'T LET ME DIE.

I CAN'T LEAVE MY KIDS ALONE.

I'M ALL THEY HAVE AFTER LOSING THEIR FATHER.

Mick decided that I was to stay captive in the room until he figured out what he was going to do with me next. In my own crazy way, I had to keep him with me so he would not go near my kids.

I was still in the process of waking up.

Mick grabbed the back of my hair, pulling me off balance. He pushed me from the front and pulled from behind down onto the chaise lounge next to our bed. Instantly with his free hand, he fixed it around my throat to exert maximum control from all sides with a white knuckle grip so I couldn't breathe at all. He was deciding just how much or how little air I was allowed to have.

I started to see stars.

This was the flashing of little lights that one perceives when on the verge of losing consciousness. There is no way to scream let alone speak. It is the most fucked up feeling in the world when someone sits on your chest and strangles you. It must be what it is like to be buried alive.

At that moment all that mattered to me was my next breath.

I pulled my right arm out and reached for his groin to squeeze whatever I could grab with all my might! His fists were now free to pound onto my face and upper body as he then jumped onto my chest to grab my throat once again.

I continued to fight back and he was sadistically amused by this and decided to jam his fingers up into my vagina to use as vicious leverage to pick me up and throw me onto the bed.

"I'm going to RAPE you now..."

He spoke as if it was a promise and a foregone conclusion.

He straddled my body and sat up as he reached for my head again. Each of his hands grabbed fistfuls of hair above my ears as he proceeded to bounce my head off the wooden headboard using the full force of his upper body. As if he was caressing a beloved, Mick used the same hands that moments before had been delivering the maximum punishment to me, to pat down the mess of my hair as if he wasn't the instrument of my torture.

One of the strange things I remember noticing is that Mick had spun strands of my blonde hair pulled freshly from my scalp still stuck to his fingers. My head was throbbing. My scalp felt hot from the extreme intensity of the pulling.

A numbing buzz came over my entire nervous system.

In a kind of loving protection and anticipation of what it knew I was about to endure, this something greater than myself was preparing me to survive whatever was to come next.

There was no way this was happening!

It can't be happening.

Oh dear God, ...

No!

No!

No!

I couldn't even remember the last time we had any intimate contact and love making in the bedroom.

When you are being raped, it's a complete takeover.

We were beyond the pale now...

As I left its form, I could actually witness the thrashing and pulling on my physical body. This was simply too much for me to endure and I had to check out. It may be when the body is traumatized there exists a defense mechanism in the form of a kind of shock, which mercifully removes us, just enough. After all that was done for the first round he sat up on me and sobbed - he reeked of fear. His agonizing tears were all he could express as the words flowed...

"Why can't you love me!?"

"We are magic together!"

These statements made by themselves are merely pathetic.

When it's uttered in the aftermath of a sexual assault, it's pathological.
He felt so sorry for himself and somehow expected me - even at this point to feel sorry for him too. The sadistic cycle would continue throughout the day until he would find himself terminally exhausted and still. Time no longer existed and

I was in a deep state of shock. All I could see in this state of numbness were the swatches of my hair tinged with blood all over our bedroom. Mick began to scurry around the room like a rat to collect them and flush them down the toilet.

Mick and I were soon pulled away from the arguing with a frantic pounding at our bedroom door. I looked at Mick for permission to answer it. He darted over to get the door before I could even get up from the bed.

In hindsight, Mick had apparently been making phone calls throughout the series of beatings to personally deliver recriminating threats to our circle of friends in anticipation of anyone who dared to intervene and help me. He stipulated they were to 'stay away and mind their own business' if they were to hear anything from me.

It wasn't long before my oldest daughter, Paige started to receive word back from our friends who were being threatened in Mick's futile attempt to control everyone and everything. Paige began to panic and ran down the hallway to try and get me out from behind the closed doors of my bedroom. She was on the outside of the threshold insanely worried about my safety. I could hear the alarm rising in her voice.

"What's going on!?!" she yelled.

I told her to 'go to her room' and that I would be fine.

Then, she pushed to open the door and before Mick could close it on her - she saw what I didn't want her to witness. Paige had caught a glimpse of my swollen bloody red face through the opening. My immediate need was to get her to go away as fast as possible for her own safety.

"Why are you bleeding mom!?

(silence)

Why is your hair so messed up?

Did HE do this to you!?!

(no reply)

Mom, ... PLEASE get out of here"!

"RUN!"

The image of the shotgun he promised to use flashed within my mind giving a clear warning to what would happen if I tried to escape. I knew this was no option and I demanded with as much authority as I could muster, that she 'get out of the house!' Paige made it down the halls into her room and soon after, her friend came to the front door. Mick managed to answer the door before my daughter and brazenly acted as if it was just a typical day - despite what she may have possibly heard from Paige.

No big deal.

Nonchalant.

The girls made their way to Paige's room clear at the other end of the 5,500 sq. foot home. Mick then stormed back into the master bedroom where I waited in fear of what was going to happen next. Mick was now aware one of my children had managed to get out of the house. He found this amusing and in the darkest way offered to give me the option to leave as well.
"Go ahead," he would threaten.

"No really, you can go." he hissed.

"It will be fun. I can chase you and you will always be looking over your shoulder waiting for me to get you. Life is like a chess game Julie ... and you know I am a master of the game. I will always be 10 steps ahead of you. I will be patient. You know me well enough to know that I can wait for years to get you when you don't expect it. This will be fun!"

"You will never escape me."

I did not move one single muscle nor can I even remember taking a breath as the horror of his words dissolved my aspirations of ever being free or happy again. I was terrified of the gun he kept in our closet as he threatened to use it if he needed to. I felt trapped and dead already. I had to do something and there was nowhere to go. So nowhere was where I stayed.

The hours that passed felt like years as I continued to stay in the room and listen to his towering rages as if they were lectures of how my life was going to be lived under his dictatorship. Blood was dripping out from my mouth and my face was now continuing to swell up. Tiny black dots were floating in front of my eyes and my ears grew numb. A high pitch ringing from a possible concussion sounded alarms in my head throughout his rampage and exhaustive beatings.

"YOU BETTER GET YOUR ASS OVER TO PAIGE RIGHT NOW AND SHUT HER THE FUCK UP, his emotional pique was in full force....

"I WILL FUCK HER SHIT UP IF SHE SAYS ONE WORD TO ANYBODY!"

I dashed out from the bedroom straight to my daughter and unfortunately her friend was sitting, now a witness inside this awful experience.

"You're, eye, ... uh, Oh My God your eye!" her friend exclaimed as she took a step back in disbelief in what she was seeing. By this time the swelling, redness, bruising and bleeding was nothing anyone could hide.

In a hush, I instructed the girls to call our family lawyer in hopes that he could calm the situation down.

Paige pleaded, in a loud stage whisper "I HAVE TO CALL THE POLICE MOM!!

WHY WON'T YOU LET ME CALL THE POLICE?

HE IS GOING TO KILL YOU!"

"You don't understand Paige! If you call the police, he will kill me for sure - and your little brother too!" By this time my youngest son was still in the home playing video games at high volume. He was blissfully unaware of the unfolding drama a few thousand square feet away.

'Please, ... just let me figure this out.' I insisted.

My beautiful and brave daughter looked at me with such confusion and frustration. I DON'T UNDERSTAND MOM!! My heart was breaking to see the disappointment and fear in her eyes as she pleaded helplessly for my cooperation. Keeping this secret was incomprehensible.

I commanded, "YOU GIRLS HAVE TO GET OUT OF HERE NOW!"

My daughter reluctantly left the house with her friend as she frantically made her volley of phone calls to the lawyer with no luck of an answer. By this time Mick had calmed himself enough to take a break from the physical exertion of the all-out abuse long enough to recover for another attack. I was then thrown onto the bed, once again, to relive the terror of another ferocious and brutal rape.

Later through the chain of evidence, I learned this attack was carried out for eight hours or more in its entirety.

It was now late afternoon. Mick made his way into the casitas outside of our house where he would change his shirt and put a fresh new one on so others would not see my blood spattered all over the old one. Back inside the bedroom, I was shut down, paralyzed and in a state of shock. It took everything I had to get myself to breathe so I could think clearly. I seized upon this moment and rallied myself to rush to the closet to remove the shotgun. Only I could not find it! My worst fear was realized as he must have taken it and hidden it from me. Now, I didn't know where to run or where to go.

My phone rang, and it was Paige. Mick gave me permission to answer as long as I was clear to her to keep her mouth shut. I will never forget the sound of her panic as she begged for permission to call the police. She thought her mother was crazy to not get the law involved. My daughter was left without any option to save her mother. Helpless and terrified, Paige proceeded to call my parents not knowing where else to turn, to come up with a strategic plan to get me out safely.

Within minutes of Mick going up into the casita over the garage the ominous sound of a helicopter coming from a great distance to then hovering in obvious circles overhead dropped me to my knees in fear that the police were indeed coming.

This was not going to be my rescue. It was going to be my execution because I knew that if Mick ever got caught, it was certain he would kill me. They can't be coming here! Dear God, please let them be going someplace else. Just pass us by... just keep going. Please.

Over the wailing of sirens approaching, the phone rang with Mick's name on the caller ID.

I answered it.

But he wasn't talking to me.

I heard him holler, "She's in the house!"... then we were cut off.

A full-on PANIC pumped through my heart. Within seconds the Sherriff's department lit up on the caller ID. Knowing they were so close now held the promise of my doom. I summoned up all my guts to answer the phone to hear a man introduce himself as one of the officers at the scene.

He proceeded to ask me to describe the floor plan of my home so that they could get me out safely.

"YOU JUST PUT THE NAIL INTO MY COFFIN!" I shouted.

"You cannot be here" I hollered. "You don't understand how powerful and dangerous this man is and he is sure to kill me if you don't leave now!"

He instructed me to just come out the front door directly. I told him my son was still in the house and I needed to get him and bring him into my room. I then ran and got my youngest boy and brought him back into my room and locked all the doors.

He repeated the directive to come out the front door. I refused. I wanted him to get my son and me from my bedroom. I wasn't going to come out the front until I knew they had Mick. "Do you have him yet!?!" "I am not coming out until you have him!"

It took a couple of minutes – during which the deputy stayed on the line with me - until finally, he could assure me they had Mick in handcuffs. "You are safe to come out now!" I remember it was so hot and bright outside. After being in the dark for so long the intensity of this daylight was overwhelming. I couldn't hardly keep my eyes open in the face of it. It wasn't my death today, it was the beginning of the rest of my life.

Mick was indeed handcuffed. Yet, he smugly rested his feet on top of the front seat of the police car. There were reports of him laughing and making friendly conversations with the officers. This terrified me that in some crazy way he was going to talk his way out of being arrested.

After they cleared the entire house I was escorted back into my home surrounded by a host of sheriff's deputies. We were now sitting around my dining room table. They were asking me questions about everything that happened. By this time they had managed to retrieve the shotgun and took pictures of the crime scene. My memories of the compassion demonstrated by these officers shall not easily be forgotten.

They seemed to be in a state of some disbelief as if they had not been exposed to a battered woman emerging from a $4 million dollar estate before. They were very professional throughout the investigation and arrest.

There was this one particular deputy, a small man, who felt it was necessary then and there to express out loud his uninvited opinions about my current situation as he helped himself to my sofa and kicked his arrogant feet up on my table.

"If I were the officer in charge ... I would tell everyone to go home!" He pronounced to nobody in particular. "Everyone is making a bigger deal out of this then need be." He continued to crow.

"That ring on your finger - is HIS ring,!" he exclaimed.
He glared directly into my eyes as if to dramatically make his point all the more clear to me. "You need to get yourselves to family therapy to sort things out!"

My response was to simply say, "Oh, you must be one of those guys that beats his wife at home and figures it's okay."

His head tilted in that strange way a dog does when it is puzzled by something it hears and can't understand. This unwanted, unwelcomed intruding officer seemed stunned that I would say any such thing back to him. Because, he appeared to be an older fellow, I immediately began to fear his recriminations if the other officers would back him up assuming he might have seniority on the younger deputies.

It turns out I was happily mistaken about that.

I look back on how fragile my situation was on so many levels.
If this insensitive bumpkin of an officer was indeed the one in charge, I could very well be dead today. Ultimately, I thank the heavens that our local police arrived in time to save my life and the lives of my precious children. There really are good and decent people in this world that want to help. However, there still is a need for more education, training and sensitivity to be aware of the stereotypes on both sides of profiling the people touched by domestic violence.

The officer who wanted to dismiss my situation out of hand was only one man convinced of how things should be for me as a 'woman of privilege'. As far as his narrow mind could see, someone like me should be beholden to the riches of rings and big fancy houses no matter what the price to pay physically.
Paige had then made her way up the long driveway towards the front door passing Officer bumpkin who was apparently still talking shit when she overheard his moronic rant about how women this well-off don't really have any problems.

"Fuck you man!"

"Get the fuck off of my driveway you piece of shit!" she commanded.

Paige walked the little man with the badge all the way down the driveway and insisted he stand on the outside of the gate.

I couldn't be more proud of my little girl.

:)

It was evident to me at that time that my stories of physical abuse were not in alignment with his - so I made a conscious choice to decide upon a kind of contrary action. Rather than cursing this fucking guy in the heat of the moment, I closed my eyes, breathed in slowly, I silently thanked him over-and-over again in my mind for his actually NOT being in charge!

The gratitude must have worked some kind of a miracle. Because, the other peace officers made clear to me at different moments and in personal asides that they each pledged to be committed to my safety. They clearly understood the severity of the situation. It is precisely because of the ones that cared enough and did their jobs well, that my family is still alive and safe today.

The shame, confusion and terror were more than I could handle while the police were asking me questions. It was hours later before Blue Julie made it to my front door followed by my parents and two of my children.

No one was allowed to touch me or even hug me for fear of disturbing the all-important physical evidence on my body and clothing.

I was still wearing my pajamas. This filthy evidence of rape and torture was ripe from so many hours of processing that I began to stink. I felt filthy and disgusting not knowing where or who to turn to for some sense of stability. The ground had been pulled out from under me and I had no one to hold me up.

I felt repulsive.

It was now 2:00 am in the morning and Blue Julie offered to take me in her car so we could follow the police to the rape clinic. The measure of a true friend is someone who is willing to endure you at your worst moment. I apologized to Blue Julie over and over on this hour long ride because I was so obviously stinking up her car with the rank aftermath of all the remnants of disgusting bodily fluids and shame that I was covered with from head to toe.

I remember it like it was a dream.

When I arrived, I must have been in an even deeper state of shock. I felt the overwhelming sting of humiliation and self-loathing when a woman came to greet us at the door at Strength United. I remember her hair was blonde and disheveled as if she had just rolled out of bed. Indeed, she had done so and was a volunteer that abandoned her precious sleep for the sake of dirty-stinky me.

This small sacrifice made a lasting impression on me. I was overwhelmed with the unfamiliar and unaccustomed feelings of being worthy enough for someone to get up for me in the wee hours of the night. I was soon led into a room to be evaluated by another woman who introduced herself as my nurse. I remember her face being very calm without a story about what she thought of me behind it.

The emotional aspect of the examination was neutral without any agenda except for the forensic evidence. I could feel a kindness in her way of being as she continued to gather her medical tools, a ruler and a camera. I was then instructed to stand on top of a clean white sheet. "Take all of your clothes off onto this blanket for evidence, … " she said. I felt humiliated and horrified! I did not want to take my robe off to feel the exposure of the shame and guilt I had brought here with me. I remember trembling and feeling very cold. But in hindsight, it may have been the trauma that was taking over. This new series of violations of my body and its privacy vibrated from my insides out.

She encouraged me to take my time and told me again that I was safe here.

She gave me a moment of privacy as she stepped a few feet away. The nurse then handed me a hospital robe to cover myself. "Let me know when you are ready." In a liquid dream state of confusion and slow motion, I managed to follow instructions to lay on the stainless steel examination table for inspection.

I laid back and looked up at the otherwise blank white ceiling. To my stunned amazement was a painted butterfly about the size of the circumference of a Folgers coffee can. This sweet image was illustrated with innocent child-like gestures with purple wings highlighted in yellow and green accents. It lifted me out of the feeling of the cold clinical procedure as my nurse proceeded to dutifully investigate all of the injuries that were evidence for the case. It was a sweet simple gesture of kindness. This silly little thing made me tear up instantly, but then everything at this time made me cry.

I don't remember how or when I got home that morning but I was instructed to go back to the clinic for further inquiry the next day. A woman approached me the moment I arrived for the second time with the eyes of compassion and concern. She introduced herself by the name of Kim Roth. She then continued to inform me that she was my advocate. I had no idea what an advocate was at that time but to ask her was going to be too exhausting at this point. I had no energy left in me. Every question she asked felt like I was running one marathon after another.

The video interview was recorded in a place called the soft room. You don't even see the camera to make it more comfortable for the subject. This testimony was then employed by all the people (*police detectives, district attorneys, etc.,*) who otherwise would have been obliged to interview me all over again. I was grateful to these people at Strength United who cared so deeply about my wellbeing to not have me relive the nightmare over-and-over again.

It didn't take long for me to feel safe with Kim and I knew she valued me as a person who deserved to be safe and respected. There was no blame or shame coming from her direction only compassion and a genuine interest in my wellbeing.

This fateful moment with the remarkably kind and compassionate Kim marked my long journey towards the beginning of the end of one life to the possibility of another.

I was literally and figuratively at the turning point.

Faith

CHAPTER 13

When do we become 'not afraid'?

$\mathcal{F}$ear: (*noun*)... an unpleasant emotion caused by the belief that someone or something is dangerous, likely to cause pain, or a threat.

Fear: (*verb*)... to be afraid of someone or something as likely to be dangerous, painful or threatening.

I never knew fear could be such a thief!

It robs us of a good night's sleep.

It hijacked my family's sense of well-being.

It cheated us out of the intimacy between mother and child.

It stole my kid's ability to have childhood friends, play sports, live in peace and feel grounded. All the things that we normally look back on with nostalgia were instead full of fear, running and hiding.

Fear left unchecked ruthlessly takes from us, our sanity.

My job was to get through the fear. Instead of remaining there I chose to get into my power - if we were ever to be free again.

Mick's arrest surprisingly did not ease the uncertainty of our futures. Mick repeatedly called me from jail. If you can believe it - he actually asked me to bail him out. His delusion was so deep he actually thought I would somehow agree *(in his words)* 'to save our relationship'. He failed to convince me even though I was afraid to deny him anything for fear of his recriminations. It was a double-edged sword for me. I was afraid to get him out and afraid not to help. Ultimately,

I decided not to help him on this.

My concern was the real possibility he would charm someone else into paying his bail.

Even after he was handed a restraining order, the futility of his polite begging continued for days. With investigators bringing forth more evidence from his past history of violence, the bail was increased from $50,000 to $500,000. By the time he got to court, the judge doubled down on Mick and set his bail for an impressive $1 million dollars.

I remember vividly being in bed at night not sleeping - trembling and breathless.

Every noise the house made at night was a possible heart stopping alarm, sounding that Mick had finally found us. I remember the children and I were always looking over our shoulders for any sign that he may have discovered our hiding place. The emotional fatigue took its toll from the effort of forcing a constant smile. Acting like we were all going to be safe was only to soothe my children into believing I knew what I was doing.

Somehow, this only provided cold comfort, knowing how angry and determined he was to kill me. We were a family in a state of shock. It took Mick around four more months to raise the $ 1 million dollars and bail himself out. This meant he was released like a predator into the wilderness that was our life at the time. I had to tell the kids we were all now on high alert. There was no point in pretending everything was normal. The kids needed to know to be extremely cautious and on the look-out.

We were forced to go into hiding full time.

I changed school districts for the kids.

We put distance between us and our past.

We changed phone numbers, bank accounts – all of that stuff.

We endured two long agonizing years of living off the grid before we had our day in court. It was critical to our survival that I continued to listen to my intuition throughout all Mick's threats and manipulative legal filings and extensions. My children were suffering, we all felt terribly isolated without our own car as we continued to arrange transportation like borrowing cars from friends and family to get them to school and back safely.

We found ourselves moving around and looking for places to live in a different country just in case he was not convicted – which was, of course, a very real possibility.

We were starting entirely from scratch on everything in our life. The simple act of buying a used car became something fraught with potential danger. The bureaucracy of the DMV is by design depersonalized. The employees working there are not professionally schooled in sensitivity training towards people like me who are the legitimate victims of domestic violence. This is obvious in terms of what I faced when they demanded my exact home address for the vehicle registration.

The way the system is currently designed, means that I would have to choose between telling the truth or risking our lives. In the end, I decided to justify compromising 'the truth' for the sake of keeping us from harm. While they were kind hearted and polite about expressing the policies – they were admittedly powerless in their position to do anything to help me even though they wanted to.

There was no leeway to give me and my kids an option to remain unexposed. At the end of the day I used my parent's address and they received all my mail for many years to come.

To bring people in the system into the reality of what my family and I were dealing with living in the conflict zone of my life - I had to restate the critical importance of not listing my real address on any records for fear of being discovered by Mick. For example, when Valencia Acura sold me a used car we had to leave the dealership without completing the purchase. Because, I simply did not have the required insurance documents in order - thanks to this exact SNAFU.

One day later, I returned with the policy in hand. I was taken aback by their kindness when they surprised me by cutting the interest on the car loan by more than half. This unexpected show of compassion for another human being instead of being just 'a customer' gave me something to be grateful for in a time of desperation. Let's be honest, car dealerships are not famous for their reputation of humanitarian gestures!

Wow.

I happily stand corrected.

Speaking of beautiful gestures, a dear friend of mine offered to rent me her home and keep all the bills in her name for the sake of our safety. There was the added comfort of knowing several active duty police officers lived on the same street. They knew my story and to watch out for us. This was a much needed silver *(and blue)* lining amongst the dark clouds over my family.

Now, I had a roof over our heads and a car for freedom of movement, yet, we were still not out of the woods. Even, the routine of the daily drive to school with the kids meant we were all wondering silently amongst ourselves if our brakes had been tampered with or some other sabotage was undertaken. This is how we would start our day - steeped in anxiety.

The kids would get dropped off in the safety of the principal's office half an hour before school. Then I would meet them again in the same office half an hour after school to avoid any confusion about who picks up my kids. It was unthinkable to allow any possibility of Mick or his possible confederates having an opportunity to grab them. Eventually, I had to homeschool my youngest daughter who was eleven at the time, She made it clear to me that there was no way she could ever feel safe away from home or from me.

We were all afraid he would find us before he went to trial. After his release for making a $1 million dollar bail in October, he could not resist calling me on his birthday in June. He darkly reminded me of what he saw as my terminal fate. I immediately called the District Attorney and returned to court to testify to his violation of the restraining order. The bail was then re-raised to $2 millon dollars and Mick was taken back into custody.

What came next literally floored me.

Six months after Mick's arrest the PTSD set in and put me completely on my ass. At the time, I had no idea what was happening to me. All I knew was my grip on reality was slipping away and it was becoming nearly impossible to function in any way that resembled normalcy. Panic attacks would override my body with anxiety. It felt like it was going to kill me! I remember being terribly alone andwithout the ability to soothe myself in the least. The adrenalin was dumping into my system daily.

The refuge I found in yoga was a saving grace.

Yet, on some days I couldn't even manage to get myself out of bed. The deep and bitter tremors of my shaking body would take me over coupled with uncontrollable sobbing, as the reality of what was really happening continued to settle in. I had done everything I could to keep this tenuous and fragile standing from my children and let them believe I was 'ok' so that they could feel safe.

This was an impossible thing to do as the family continued to unravel without the stability of another parent to lean on. Kim Roth, my advocate and counselor from Strength United never judged me. She had made a commitment to never leave or disrespect my journey. She took our situation very seriously and reminded me on repeated occasions that what I was experiencing was not unusual. She was my sanctuary and I love her with all my heart! Kim continued to remind me of my intuitive voice, of a higher power and all the strength it gave me throughout this journey. It felt like there was nothing that was going to take me out of this depression - so I did what I knew worked best.

I went IN.

After several weeks of trying to comprehend what I was experiencing, I told my children that I was going to be in my room if they needed me. This wasn't too unusual in itself as I spent much time in my room alone anyway. But this time was going to be different. I was on a mission to open the chamber of hell and have a face-off with the demons that were waiting for me on the other side.

I got down onto my knees and asked for guidance from the wisdom I knew that had taken me this far and had always spoken the truth. 'Quiet' was the silent message that laid me down onto the floor as I looked up at the blank white ceiling.

No butterflies here.

My body began to shake with a ferocity that literally pounded my bones onto the carpet. The cold sweats showed no mercy to my calling for a truce. With undeniable faith, I stayed there and let the energy flow through me as I watched my thoughts try to attach themselves to the stories that brought me here.
There was nowhere to run and no one else to carry my pain for me. I let go of the resistance that was calling me away from this new frontier. To describe it as some kind of uncomfortable moment would be an absurd understatement. I HEAR YOU - I FEEL YOU were the words spoken from me - to the fear. I didn't want to run anymore, I knew this was the only way for me to allow the sensation to be witnessed and released. I was not going to fight against this pain any longer, so I surrendered to the wisdom of my own body and felt her process.

DO WHAT YOU HAVE TO DO.

Be still.

Listen.

I was not going to interfere anymore.

The pain was intense and the stories continued to torment me. The adrenaline continued to protect me from the danger of the past as my sympathetic nervous system was still stuck in high gear. It needed time to process and release the momentum that had been collecting after all those years of abuse and stress. I knew if I could just be patient and let it pass without resistance, it would have to eventually slow down. After all, it was only there for my survival and it was going to do its job until it didn't feel the threat any longer.

My mind and my body needed to catch up with each other so one of us had to be the one to surrender and wait. 'Whatever doesn't kill you only makes you stronger' is a familiar phrase yet death felt like it would have been a tempting escape and relief from my reality at that moment. I had not realized how much trauma my body had actually taken in. I was busy trying to stay alive and cope with the day to day terror. What I didn't know was my fear was being buried in places where I got hurt.

I know this had a purpose and I'm grateful for the native intelligence that takes over and watches out for us when we are no longer able to think clearly. Now was the time to set it free and not tangle it up with my attachment to the false and cruel opinions of myself.

Three days had now passed.

A tumultuous storm had ravaged through my body. The energy was beginning to soften. As the emotional tide retreated - I was wiped out. It left me with a strange sensation of calm which I recognized with great appreciation as genuine relief. It was time for me to ask myself who I would be without all the violence and horrible memories of the past. It was difficult to imagine, yet I continued to practice the feeling of who I would be if my story was different. I was certain of how it felt to be a victim of repeated assault and what kind of a life I was living as an abused woman.

I felt a passionate calling for a life of peace.

The person I became in the aftermath was utterly unable to co-exist with who I was when living in violence. The solace I was so desperate for was most present when I was committed to my daily meditations and yoga practice.

I did all that I could do and that had to be enough.

Even the days that held me down in grief had some value by recognizing they were a much needed call for rest and release. As I began to understand the pain as a part of my process to heal, the reaction to push it away became less intense and the experiences of agony gently decreased as the days passed. To understand more deeply, this meant the grief gave me the ability to use it as a guidance process instead of making it my enemy.

I was dedicated to paying close attention to its message so I could use that revelation to help navigate my mind. The hardest thing for me personally at the time, was to find hopeful and positive thoughts and not to feed into the fear for too long. It's like being stuck in traffic and there is nowhere to go but where you are at that time. We can struggle and fight against it and still go nowhere.

The only thing we seemed to accomplish with any success when stuck is the state of misery and discomfort we are now experiencing. If we just take a breath and know that we won't be trapped in the experience forever, we may gently guide our minds and emotions to a place of more acceptance. The traffic begins to move forward again and in time you will be free from the anguish of feeling held like a prisoner. Not even a million stopped cars around you can hold you captive in your mind!

To be free is a blessed state of being.

We know this to be true, because the moment we feel imprisoned or victimized, we begin to suffer! We unknowingly serve the temptation to take ourselves to the dark chattering thoughts, our inner voice is always speaking yet we cannot hear her. We silence the voice of wisdom in ourselves and continue to discredit her existence. We feel abandoned and betrayed, yet it is US that feeds into the torture through our misguided beliefs and projections.

We imprison our own selves simply by the way we think. There is wisdom in chaos and pain. This very real and uncomfortable sensation is our guide telling us we are moving further away from our higher intuition.

Can suffering be considered a friend? I say yes.

It can because it gives me the clarity to recognize the moments when I have forgotten something that is true about myself. The God I know to be real is forever speaking to me and now I know when I am not listening.

Acceptance

CHAPTER 14
Self-rule of Freedom

*A*s a child growing up, I did not have a good relationship with anger. The house I was raised in, to be angry, showed weakness or at the very least being guilty of being the one without reason. Where does all the energy go when we stuff the rage away, deep inside the back of our minds?

What is it? Where does it come from? Is it a real thing? Do we speculate to protect ourselves from others that do us wrong?

The house I was born into was not a violent home nor was there ever permission to argue with one another if we felt an injustice was done. If an expression of anger were to be released openly, it seemed as though the sky would fall and bury us into the flaming abyss of hell! As far as my young mind was concerned, there was no way I was going to go to hell. Instead, I resisted the anger – no matter what happened - and soon became so disconnected that I could no longer identify with what an authentic angry feeling was.

Did I have the right to feel the way I did when I was frightened or frustrated? I suppose I did, but, I certainly wasn't willing to suffer the consequences for it. In a way, I did live in a violent home, silently. People that have had the unfortunate experience of being raised in an environment where their families expressed anger through violence may say that I was the lucky one to not have been exposed to an environment filled with screaming and hitting. Indeed, this is true, yet the rage was without an identity or an outlet for me.

It didn't matter if someone was bullying me, because I wasn't allowed to get angry in a way I felt I could defend myself. I shut off from ever going there with myself, because I would feel ashamed. I realized later in life my boundaries were non-existent and it made me an open target for others to come in and get their own aggressions out without consequence. Yes, I was a great big giant victim screaming out for others to abuse! Go ahead, please, I will be happy to be the one to receive your insanity so that I can somehow process my own!

All of this taught how to avoid conflict and stay as far away from angry thoughts as possible. I wasn't going to allow myself to believe anger existed at all - at least not within me. That was the curse for others to experience. I was going to have none of it. Throughout my life there have been so many episodes of bullying and abuse and yet here I was filling up my 'denial file' in my mind until the thing got so big I thought my head would explode!

Is it possible to be a person of peace and not have some kind of a relationship with anger? If anger and rage didn't exist, then how will I ever have the range of emotion and contrast to even know the difference?

The time had come for me to get pissed off!

But the thing is, I needed to know I was safe *(and sane)* throughout the experience. There was a flat out war going on inside. My intuition told me it was time to unleash the energy that I held captive for so long. By practicing the concept of doing 'harm to none' would be the only way to unleash the monster within me without feeding the fire and contaminating others.

What would happen if I spoke up, told my truth and actually say NO to someone?

Maybe that person would decide they didn't like me anymore. Worse, they could confirm what they already suspected they didn't like about me. Dear God. What would happen if I was wrong and then left with the shame of being angry for the wrong reasons?

There is no other way to develop a relationship with anyone including ourselves until we go there and explore how we relate to anger and know it is strictly an emotion that we believe in. Anger can be a force to harm if we believe in its power and forget our own higher power. We always try to run from it, but it will relentlessly figure out a way to find us.

The enormous energy generated by anger provides a way to strive towards what is important. On the other hand, if we deny the power as if it does not exist we allow it to cripple ourselves. When I am oblivious to emotions I can get tangled up in the narrative. Instead of using the energy to drive to something useful then most likely I shall fall victim to the rage.

For example, if I take the time to be mindful when I am angry, I can then show up for the experience to determine and discriminate what is real and what is not. In the past, I have made a habit of stuffing it away and calling out to others subconsciously to bring it to life for me. Either way, this uncomfortable emotion is insisting that I notice it. If I choose to make it my enemy, will it take over and destroy my life?

It wasn't until I took a step back from it to realize it already had.

The fact that I ignored my own personal feelings of anger made it more alive than ever! I was holding myself back from recognizing the inner voice of love and reason because it fell into a wild, wild sea . . . lost within the waves of rage. Was it possible to love and trust myself enough to experience the conflict, yet still be a good, decent and even peaceful person?

When conflict continues to knock on our door, do we open it or pretend we don't hear it? There is no question the door is knocking. What is it we are so afraid of? Is it me that I fear when I am face to face with it, or the terror of the unknown? The mystery waits for us within a formless and dark uncertainty. We don't perhaps feel the sense of confidence that we are going to be safe if we dare go there. What happens if we muster up the courage to find out?

The relentless knocking at the door never goes away.

We choose to suffer through the anxiety and ignore it. Soon, we are in an obsessive panic! Good lord, just open the fucking door and get rid of the misery!

After all the resistance, torture and fear we reluctantly open-up to the secret that has been calling us for so long. A desperate need, in terms of relief, is no longer able to resist itself as it embraces this intimate moment with you. There is nothing to lose at this point, because the anticipatory turmoil has taken all of the energy we once had to fight against it.

We reach for the handle with hesitation. There is no turning back now. Go ahead, turn it, do it, get it over with! Unfasten the door to a wide-open space of obscurity where all your personal demons live. We have already come this far, we may as well open our eyes to see what fear looks like. Our fainthearted mind's eye refuses to open as the space remains empty. Curiosity carries our feet forward deeper into the unknown. We call out to the personalized demons to secure our surroundings with their reactions.

All we hear is a deafening silence.

We move deeper and further away from the safe place we ventured in from. Our ears can no longer tolerate the quietude and our eyes become dissatisfied with the total absence of anything comforting. We stand there almost disappointed. We are at the end of a long anticipated journey, only to meet up with no one there but ourselves.

Habitual shame has nothing to attach itself to here. There is no one to point the finger at or to even run away from. These specters aren't even there to own up to the excuses of our mistakes or even hold responsibility for the guilt we want to rid ourselves of. Look what we do to ourselves. All the time and energy we invest into the fear of these nightmares proves to be a waste of time in terms of self-torment.

In my denial, I became sick and depressed.

What appeared to be a punishment in regards to my pain, discomfort and sickness was just the wisdom of my body loving me, refusing to believe in the dysfunction as it called out for my attention. What was I going to do with this new embracing of my inner rage now? At this point, I am sick, underweight, and suicidal. If nothing else, this made matters worse and it was not filling me with much hope. Unknowingly, I had given permission to the stuffed up anger to consume and kill me on the installment plan. I was in denial of my own self-worth. I realized I didn't even believe I had the permission to be pissed off! Is this a battle that needs to take place for my sanity and happiness? In fact, this process is a wonderful gift and certainly not the curse that I once thought it to be.

The source of who I really am, is not capable of existing in the dysfunction of turbulence and chaos. The perception of fear is my compass spinning away from my true North.

Why would I continue to hide or stuff the anger down when it is the very thing that is guiding me back to myself? I am learning to pay closer attention to the emotions of anger as they lovingly remind me that I am trailing away from my own eternal verities. Feeling it, allowing the sensation to process without feeding into it gives anger a profound intimacy. When something isn't right, or I am not understanding myself correctly within a situation, these cues have become a personal kind of reliable guidance system.

A tremendous amount of energy is thrusting our emotions outwards when we are aggravated. To think that we stuff these powerful emotions down or even radiate them onto others is the very thing we do that keeps us so miserable. The only thing that seems real when we become angry is confusion.

What are we so confused about?

Perhaps, this uncomfortable emotion can be used as our guidance system instead of being considered a curse. Imagine how often our hearts beat rapidly, our hands and legs begin to shake when the adrenalin has taken over. We must do something with all of this energy or we will implode! To unleash it out on the world through ignorance only creates more violence. We ourselves are in danger of becoming the hypocrites we accuse others of being.

We choose to be the masters behind the violence or the masters of peace.

When I feel the discomfort of bitterness or resentment, I immediately suffer. If I continue to cradle and nurture this emotion with pride and fall into the illusion that 'I am the victim' it grows and becomes my reality. When in truth, suffering is the very gift given to us to recognize that it is we that separated ourselves from the magnificent higher beings we truly are. What a fantastic and loving gift to hold this wisdom to be self-evident.

We are the majesties in our own minds!

When we know someone is projecting an opinion of himself or herself upon us and we refuse to believe in it, the projection loses all of its power to affect us. If someone were to tell me, I had blue eyes and they believe blue eyes are a curse - how could I even embrace that thought when I know that I have brown eyes? This is evidence that we cannot fall victim to others pain if we don't believe somehow or someway that their pain is our pain too.

The most powerful shape shifters on this planet are the people that have a healthy relationship with their higher selves and put their energy into the solution - not the problem.

We cannot heal suffering with more suffering.

We cannot heal anger with more anger.

We cannot heal violence with more violence.

The door will continue to annoy you with its relentless pounding and increase the chaos within us if we refuse the call to our courage and trust ourselves to open it. No one will be there on the other side to greet you but yourself, I promise. Perhaps this is the wisdom that terrifies us the most. There will be no one to blame, no one to play "the bad guy" or take responsibility for our suffering, but us. The discharge of this realization is quite liberating. I can't think of a more beautiful way to describe the freedom of self-rule.

Courage

CHAPTER 15
The truth will be told the night before the trial:

*O*ur future was uncertain.

After countless delays, the time had finally arrived for our day in court. Only 12 hours away and I must face the man that repeatedly beat, threatened, and raped me over the course of several years. Honestly, I didn't know how I was going to survive the moment when I would feel his eyes piercing through my body with his rage, while plotting his revenge. The anticipation was more than I could handle. My throat started to tighten. My body literally shook uncontrollably with dread. I became unable to hear or see anyone around me.

All I wanted to do was run!

At the time, my entire body was unhinged and uncertain. It seemed incomprehensible that our lives were now going to be in the hands of 12 complete strangers whom I had never met before. Through peaks and valleys of emotion, I had to get through the trial, but it felt to me like a death and dying process.

Would this random group of jurors somehow have the ability to see through the deceit of this irresistibly charming sociopath and set us free? The thought of being in the same room with him . . . triggered me massively.

I can remember pleading with God, asking for a glimpse of clarity as to why all this was happening inside me. I needed reassurance to know I was not going to be abandoned and left alone to face the wolves in Mick's den who wanted to rip me apart and destroy me in court. I found myself blinded by fear and feeling altogether helpless. I had to be mindful not to fall into this self-imposed trap within my own thoughts.

The night before the trial began, I made my way into the privacy of my bathroom, to have a good cry. My sobbing face was pitifully covered in snot and tears to the point where I could hardly get a breath in. I remember calling out to God,

"What do You want from me?"

How will I ever be able to compete in a courtroom with this charming man who is so utterly convincing and resourceful? After all, his cunning mind was more than capable of convincing me to deeply question my own sanity. Would he be able to do the same with the jury?

The only thing I was sure of now was that I was falling apart. I needed God to tell me what to do. I closed the door and sat on the cold tile floor. My breakdown came to a sudden halt.

"JUST TELL THE TRUTH!"

This was all I could hear through the distraught extremes I had retreated to. Somehow, this man had the uncanny ability to turn a lie into a beautiful opportunity to get everything he wanted in the past. If I tell the truth now, he will most certainly find a way to make it seem like a lie.

"TELL YOUR TRUTH!"
The clarity started to set in. I realized I didn't even know what my truth was. I had been living a life based on coping within an unsustainable violence. Mick wanted to control every single thing in my existence. My struggle for survival had produced the causes and conditions of confusion for who " I " really was in all of this noise.

In the past, Mick had the skills to manipulate me and twist things around to get what he wanted. I believed I was not capable of competing with such a perverse intelligence. If I were to know what my truth was, I would have to turn inward. After several breaths, I felt a blanket of calm drape over me, enveloping my underweight and fragile body. The grounding of simply sitting on terra firma helped stabilize me and my turbulent emotions.

There she was.

My higher voice called confident and certain.

"GET UP, I've got you."

Honestly, I don't recall sleeping at all that night ... but, the sun did rise the next day.
The trial was about to begin.

Truth

CHAPTER 16
Day one of the trial:

$\mathcal{T}$he sky was clear.

Everything looked so vivid and motionless. I reminded myself to breathe and be mindful of where my thoughts were taking me. Deliberately, I selected soothing music for our drive to the courthouse. As the discovery process unfolded over the previous two years, I was introduced by the D.A. to several of the women that were on the receiving end of violence from the same man in my life. Escorted by the police into a safe room, it became apparent I wasn't the only one that was scared to death of Mick.

I was taken aback when reprimanded and 'How dare you'd' by one of the women in particular as result of her panic. Her fear was, Mick would retaliate against her because of this. It was interesting how easily I became labeled as the troublemaker and the one to be held responsible for what might happen to these women and their children if I continued with my testimony.

As much as I would have loved to make it all go away and take the experiences to my grave, MY TRUTH simply would not be compromised. In this safe space, I explained to them that I could not live with myself or sleep at night knowing that this man would be free to destroy other innocent lives - if I hadn't found the courage to do the right thing. It was clear to everyone there that all these women (*including myself*) would not have had to go through this shit - if just one of the previous had found the courage inside herself before the next woman.

Look how many women are in this room because nobody did anything.

I refused to become part of the legacy of the secret by not taking right action.

We were all acutely aware of how we were not allowed to discuss any of the details relating to the case or any testimony with one another until after the trial was over - but we did offer an unspoken sense of sisterhood to give each of us the support we needed within our court imposed vows of silence.

The trial was scheduled for 14 days.

Three of my children, my parents and several friends were called to testify. Mick had a list of people lined up to testify against my good character and try to paint me as a superficial conniving gold digger. It was frustrating as hell as the list of names surfaced on his behalf. It was astonishing to even think for a moment these witnesses could be so completely fooled. I was beginning to see how the shame and 'secrets of violence' were working against me.

Something in the back of my mind scolded, "Why didn't you say something sooner?"

How could they believe in speaking such lies when they never once had a personal falling out with me? I wondered to myself what mental gymnastics they were performing inside of their head to justify lining up as witnesses for the defense. We heard behind the scenes reports of financial deal sweeteners that were taking place, just to get testimonies in line with his strategy to flip the script and make him somehow the victim in all of this.

Didn't the witnesses care about my children at the very least? The kids were innocent little lives that could have been killed as a result of their petty collaboration. This is not a game. This is a battle for our lives. There was nothing I could have gained from my bearing false witness by making up a story of abuse.

It's disheartening to watch people abandon victims of violence. The only answer I could begin to understand at this point, was to accept these people had no idea what they were doing. What would allow them to realize the severity of what consequences their alignment with the then alleged abuser meant? Perhaps they had an axe to grind with someone else who resembled me in some fashion that triggered their own anger. All I knew was that I had only myself to rely upon to keep things straight and let the truth be told – independent from any master manipulator polluting my thoughts.

When victims of crime go to trial and experience the opposing side coming at them, it is an assault on the senses and another form of violence for them to experience. Just when you think you are going to be safe because the threat has been removed from your home, you are expected to endure the civilized version of courtroom warfare. Defense lawyers circle the witness stand with both barrels loaded coming at you with all the guile of assassins. They blast away at your character trying to shoot down your credibility. In my experience, this process of cross-examination had all the subtlety of repairing a fender-bender by way of swinging a giant wrecking ball from a crane to smooth out a scratch in your paint.

Total broadsides.

I knew I had to retreat to the sacred space within my mind where God provided me a refuge where it was safe to hear what Mick had to say to me through his lawyers since he did not end up testifying himself.

(Mick nearly resorted to taking the stand to testify on behalf of his own defense in desperation – despite the legal advice of his counsel)

When things become unbearable, we tend to find ourselves on our knees pleading to the almighty for his or her mercy. We come up with this idea that we have been left and forgotten. Maybe, we did something so unforgivable that we are now being punished and having our faith tested? If God is LOVE and truth - why do we suffer?

Why do bad things happen to good people?
I have come to understand for myself that when I cry out to God – it isn't him or her that has abandoned me and then suddenly remembers where I am – it's myself that recognizes the higher power that has been there all along. How can God be in the light and the darkness at the same time? Where there is love, God will be there too. Maybe this is why we feel so alone when we suffer? We somehow tend to believe more in the suffering itself than we do in the true nature of who we are.

Yes, here it is. THE TRUTH.

It's up to me to seek the clarity through the lens of higher consciousness, not through the perception of those who perpetuate evil, confusion and the fear it cultivates. I found that this awareness is the gift that set me free. I needed to remind myself of this constantly throughout the trial. I held on to keeping the quality of my mind calm and clear. This was not an easy thing to do in the grips of intimidation through the impersonal process of the trial. I knew this experience was not just about me anymore. This was also about Mick, his family and their history as well.

This was something the judge, the lawyers and the jury were all showing up for in their own lives. I worked diligently on where I was allowing my thoughts to roam. I knew if I continued to be a citizen participant in the landscape of fear – it would always find a way to take me down one way or another.

How was I going to clean up this shit storm?

I realized the more I focused on him, I would be calling forth a belief within myself that was not true. Therefore, in a strange way, I thanked him. Mick had shown me who I really can be – and whom I never want to return to being again. What direction did I want the intolerance to take me? What was I avoiding in the moment to create such confusion? I had become a master of survival yet felt clueless in hectic moments of chaos when I was asked to do the very thing that would set me free.

I knew today was going to be the beginning of a new challenge. Then, I made a promise to myself that I would be mindful and honest, no matter how badly the truth became twisted. I knew the moment I became entangled within the fear and confusion, I would be lost again. It was not going to be easy. However, I had to go back to the time when I realized what was really happening here. I was only going to find that freedom and safety in my mind. These were the kinds of things I had learned through the history of my relationship with Mick. Neither he nor anyone else in the courtroom, could take that away from me.

I knew this was the key for me to now live my life from here on in. I became a student of my surroundings and the people within it, willing to listen and learn. I made a commitment that I would be mindful not to get caught up in the caricature they were creating me to be and to see his attorney as a beautiful human being that chose to be a student too. I know they wanted to get into my head and browbeat me into buying into their scare tactics.

Whatever happens, the final decision to be made about our future was not my responsibility. I had to let that go. Otherwise, I would have lost my way. I found myself capturing the haunting thoughts that would creep in,

He is going to kill you and your children.

He is going to get away with this.

No one is going to believe you.

Everyone here thinks you are a bad vindictive person and he is the true victim.

Over and over again, I would catch myself from falling into the false identity that he and his lawyer wanted to portray to the jury.

The judge would say, "hold on, ... she's meditating again." For some reason the moment I would pause to take a breath and clear my mind, the judge actually noticed. I found his insight refreshing and even a little bit funny. It gave me a sense of assurance that I could take my time and not be bulldozed by the defense. Oddly enough, Mick's lawyer tried to turn the conversation about yoga against me many times throughout the trial. Ironically, she would remind me several times of the mantra Abyasa/Viragya without even knowing it. (*This is a Sanskrit message to take action towards the path of truth and let go of attachments and grasping to the outcome*).

Mick's lawyer would talk quickly at me with overwhelming energy of anger and disgust. I found myself in defense mode many times within the beginning of my three day testimony. She managed to shake me up a bit as she would skillfully rattle me with her accusations and confuse me with my own answers. I started to catch my breath and tell her that I loved her in the privacy of my mind so I could find a place to calm myself. *(I admit, this took some practice as she made it hard for me to love her over and over again).*

I knew what she was doing and she did it well. However, there is nothing that can discredit the truth and it was going to be up to me to stay in a place within myself, so I could hear it over her intimidating tactics. Regardless of how it appeared, I was the one with the power to speak it, not her. I was the one that was beaten, raped and tortured - not her. I knew all the details, so it was up to me to expose the evidence.

My senses became heightened during this process so much so that my ears could pick up the whispering and nasty comments coming from the supporters of the defendant. "They do not know the truth", was what I had to remind myself, over and over. The judge ordered them to silence themselves. I could see Mick offering looks to the jury silently asking them to set him free. It was so blatant to me that I had to turn away physically from his obvious attempt to sway the jury. Still vulnerable, I knew if I looked at him directly I might fall apart emotionally, so I chose not to.

"Admit it – you were the one who was using him for his money and you made this whole story up to get what you wanted!"

You are an evil conniving bitch who has no heart and no conscious – he is the real victim here! We are going to chew you up and spit you out!. These were the paralyzing sentiments spoken and unspoken to me in a room of influential listeners. It was up to me to inform the jury about what the situation was really - in stark contrast to the tilted portrayal of Mick's defense team.

Justice

CHAPTER 17
The final days in Court

May 5 th 2010.

This was the final day for the witnesses to be heard in court.

All sides were exhausted and stressed. The uncertainty of the outcome was taking its toll on all of us. The mystical knowledge of my reality was apparent to me even then - that we all had our own unique and individual paths to live after the announcement of the verdict. I knew it wasn't my place to hope for a cruel and long punishment for Mick, but after all ... who was I to determine what was best for him?

All I knew was I had to tell the truth and release the secrets that contaminated so many innocent lives. The brutality was sure to continue on if this man were to walk out of the courtroom free to practice his habits of violence. Personally, I wanted nothing more than to be free of Mick and live my life without him in it. Imagining time with my children without the phantom of our past was my preferred place of refuge. We could put the pieces of our family back together again - given half the chance.

The thought of enjoying something as simple as a family BBQ and having friends over without Mick's tantrums was something to actually look forward to. The idea of my kids and I going somewhere together and spending time as a family uninterrupted by a controlling and cruel dominating atmosphere was opening my heart. We were gently reminding one another how wonderful it felt to be hugged, or to carry a conversation with one another without Mick yelling, screaming and barging around with his jealousy.

It had been a long agonizing journey for all of us and it was time for it to end. We were at the mercy of 12 men and women who carried their own personal stories and beliefs when it came to violence. This was a vulnerable and uncertain space for my kids and me to be in. All we could do at this point was wait…and wonder.

After 12 long gut-wrenching days, the lawyers had now finished their questioning and it was time for the jury to decide. Mick began to panic knowing things were not going very well for him. He was a monster and the evidence of that was presented within the courtroom exposing him for what he had wrought. He began to panic. Mick stalled the proceedings while firing his attorney and asking the Judge for advice if he should choose to go up onto the stand to testify on his own behalf. I watched this man who had for many years managed to appear smarter than everyone else in the same room and was always far more willing to do whatever it took to get what he wanted - begin to unravel.

The show was now coming to an end. All the desperate attempts to discredit my character had all been exhausted by Mick's lawyer as she desperately tried to paint me as a horrible liar. I found myself feeling trapped on many questions because the truth was not being put to light correctly. The truth, in this case, proved itself to be impenetrable and it always found its way back to the courtroom even when it appeared it was being deliberately and professionally twisted and buried. They had run out of theories to discredit my character and his lawyer went as far as to tell the jury a story about an innocent boy and a violent, deceitful wolf that tricked the boy and destroyed his life. Yes, I was the Big Bad Wolf in the fairy tale and Mick was the sweet and innocent caring boy.

We didn't wait for long for the verdict to come in.

(three hours later)

The right side of the courtroom where the jury sits was buzzing with anticipation of their freedom as the left side of the courtroom where the defendant was seated were praying for the same thing. Here we all were, hoping for the same outcome - to be set free, yet the two sides were on opposite ends of the spectrum.

One last dramatic moment of truth.

Will Mick be set free so my children and I have to make our escape once again? Are we going back to the fear that of his retaliations? Or, … will we be set free from this nightmare and have the time and space to heal into a better more joyful life?

The anticipation was intense and to witness Mick and his family in desperation was mind-blowing. They would stand in a circle together in the hallway and hold a King James Bible in the air and pray out loud. It was quite a performance to watch him and I was not amused. Mick had never taken any interest in religion. I knew him to take pleasure in mocking others in the past who were genuinely sincere in their faith. I knew better that this performance was some sort of bizarre theater being played out and it was embarrassingly obvious to those of us that knew him. He would stop at nothing to win. It was in his nature to perform and manipulate.

This was his final desperate attempt to sway the jury so they may see him in a better light while waiting in the hallway of the courtroom... or maybe he miraculously found God in the dark night of his soul during recess?

The verdict was ready to be announced.

At this time, I felt the hands of my loved ones touching me in reassurance that I was not alone. I grabbed my mother's hand and reached over the chair in front of me to grab Paige's hand as we all waited for our fate to be announced.

"First count of felony rape ......GUILTY! "

I felt an immediate surge of relief thrust through my body as it lifted me right out of my seat.

"Second count of felony rape.... GUILTY!

Tears of sweet justice and freedom trailed down the faces of all those concerned about their own lives. The other women and children now had the same hope I had to live their lives without the paralyzing fear of this charming, dangerous and deadly man ever hurting them again.

"Third count of criminal threats... GUILTY! "

It felt as if I had won the largest lottery in the world! This was a result beyond measure in any dollar amount.

"Fourth count of previously convicted felon with a firearm.... GUILTY! "

The courtroom was beginning to accumulate a discord of energy as the emotions from one side of the room to the other side of the room clashed in fierce polarity.

"Fifth count of felony sexual penetration by a foreign object ... GUILTY! "

My eyes could no longer focus as my heart opened to the light that promised me and my children a new and peaceful future!!! I could hardly recognize myself or him within the newness of this precise moment. All the accumulated threats and abuse were going to be put to an end right here and now. I was no longer buried deep within the secrets where the monsters lived blinding me from my truth any longer. My higher voice was sweet and comforting as if she knew the outcome of this nightmare all along. I found myself concerned for his future for a brief moment.

I caught myself getting involved in his story – as if it were any of my business . . .

Mick was sentenced to 24 years without the possibility of parole in a maximum security state penitentiary. My realization was he too has a path that has been chosen by him and his relationship to the divine. It was his life to be in prison or to have chosen another way. Perhaps this way was in his best interest as well.

I can only speculate and wonder . . .

How?

When?

Why?

What?

Yet, I choose to stay within my own stories that I will continue to write about a free and happy life for my kids and myself.

I'm very thankful for "The People" of Los Angeles for showing up to do the right thing and for doing their part in keeping people safe. I am aware not all stories end as well as mine did, so I speak from my own experience in hopes that truth and justice answer to all those who call out to her.

"self-deceptions cannot take the place of truth"
~ a course in miracles

Empowerment

CHAPTER 18

A Tribute to my Teachers
Don't judge me by my past! I don't live there anymore.
~ author unknown

*S*everal years have now passed since I found myself living in fear of my former partner in violence. Looking back on my life, I see how frightened I was every single day of that previous existence. I can't help but notice the contrast between then and now.

Would I know myself as I do today without the experiences and the lessons from my past?

I can look back with a heart filled with regret and shame if I so choose, or rather, I can think about how freedom feels in this moment. I'm grateful for all the lessons and opportunities that have been gifted to me even through the grim and dramatic events years ago. There is a new sense of freedom when we take control of our own lives with a consciously responsible mindset.

This is a new awareness.

Who am I after all the horror and violence?

Now, I live a life in a peaceful home with my husband and our seven children. It took several years for me to pull myself from the attachment to previous beliefs by changing my old convictions into a new way of knowing that a relationship could offer me safety, harmony and respect. All four of my kids are now adults and we continue to work together as a family. It has been a rough ride throughout the years and each one of us has had our own unique way of processing the pain.

The greatest wake-up call was realizing that my children can feel the shift in me. They have a mother who is more present and supportive. Today, I can sit and enjoy deep conversations with my loved ones and listen to what they are saying with great interest from me. There were many years when I was unable to process and sit long enough to hear what the other person would be saying to me. My mind would wander off and the anxiety I was experiencing robbed from us all the personal mother to child intimacy. My children have been gifted with the return of their mother and I have been privileged with the honor and joy of being there for my babies.

People often ask me if I think about Mick and all the suffering he may be now experiencing. I made a conscious decision to release my anger without consequence to anyone - so the violence wouldn't spread and grow. I had to get real with myself and take responsibility for my choices and perceptions about the relationship, so I could free myself of the obsession towards his punishment.

The anger was not able to surface until the shock and depression processed first. I made a commitment to let others help me knowing that the isolation I once experienced kept me uninformed and unsupported. My commitment consisted of weekly therapy, writing, reading and yoga. I knew I needed to metabolize the immense reservoir of energy that accumulated over all the years of violence before I could begin to see myself as a free woman.

I realized that to be truly liberated it would be necessary to forgive him somehow and more importantly... to forgive myself. The process showed me what was essential to working my way back to a life free of the entanglements of the past. In a strange way, the act of forgiving him was easy because I had no reason to hold him responsible after I owned up to the experience myself.

The true meaning of freedom is - it begins with me.

Someone once asked me what I would say to him if I were to ever have the opportunity. My response would be something like this...

Mick, ...Thank you for hearing my desperate, silent cries of rage and for showing up to share in the experience with me. I did not know how to live with myself because I was clearly shut off from the source of love that I now know myself to be. I needed you to give me an excuse to blame someone else for my misery and pain. Back then, I did not know how to look inside for the answers I was so desperate to find. I love you for allowing me to reflect your own terrors so that we both could share in our pain together.

The truth is, I felt I was unable to carry the burdens of my own life without the outlet you offered me. I could not see this without putting the blame onto you because it was unbearable to withstand myself if I had to take responsibility for my own confusion. I needed you to convince me that I mattered to someone and that I was worthy of love. Instead, you unleashed my worst fears and gave me the opportunity to see for myself how real or not real they really were. I'm grateful for our sacred relationship even though it was a horrible and painful one. You helped in showing me exactly who I then believed Julie to be. We came together as lost souls forgetting to be whole and true to the love of our own selves. We continued to torment one another perhaps not understanding why at the time. Yet I so desperately needed you to show me I was more than a lost and forgotten women. You fulfilled your part of the bargain by being who you were as a lonely, frightened young man. I too validated the pain as the victim that feeds on only the weakness of a sleeping consciousness.

Our egos played together and competed to a point where they almost killed us both. It is evident to me now that I was willing to accept whatever someone was willing to offer just to feel loved. I want you to know that I take full responsibility for the woman I showed up as when we came together. I was a desperate partner that didn't even realize the suffering and agony I was holding onto inside. I needed you to soothe my ego so I could be convinced of my worthiness. I also take responsibility for the woman I now know myself to be today.

I am a woman willing to find the courage to look inside even if it means I have to feel the discomfort of owning up to my own life experience. I would not have had the ability to discover this awareness without the contrast of love and fear within our courtship. I am now free to decide for myself if I am going to be a victim or a thriving, resilient woman. I had been unaware that I always had this choice until I had to get real with Julie and call out to "my higher voice" to understand how loved I truly am. I could never have received this gift from you without putting in the effort to see things differently about myself. I had been focusing all of my attention and self-love onto you and your pain, for that I am truly sorry.
How was I ever going to expect you to fulfill the expectation of true happiness if neither one of us had a clue what it was in the first place? How selfish it was of me to make demands of you to be peaceful when you didn't know how to release your own pain. Our expectations of one another left us both so unhappy and with only ourselves to investigate.

The longer we ignored the wisdom of self-reflection - the more violent the relationship became.

I want you to know that I forgive you for abandoning me and for all the pain you have caused in my life!

I also want you to know that I forgive ME for abandoning ME and for all the pain I have caused in MY life!"

Now our business together is done.

Perhaps forgiveness is the first step in understanding which can lead to a deeper knowing.

I now understand that to be free and happy I need to do the work on my own thinking and beliefs first. I then can be well aware of who I am before I show up to anything and for anyone in my life.

If I am suffering, I will call for more suffering.

I chose not to blame another for showing up the same way I did.
We will never *(ever)* know our own power and worth if we continue to point the finger at others and blame them for our pain and claim ourselves as victims!

When we keep secrets for others that hurt and abuse people we are feeding into the violence. Who does this make us if we continue to practice the enabling of others? The big fat ugly secret of domestic and sexual abuse is slowly leaking out nowadays from the ones whom have found their courage to be free of the victim mentality.

This is commendable and beautiful because ALL parties involved are now set free from the anguish of secrets and lies.

We are not only here to show up for the ones we want to label as the victims. We also need to face the monsters that feed on the same fear that the perpetrators are living in as well. I'm not saying for one second that those that choose to hurt others should be set free and be dismissed. Their future and spiritual journey very well may be calling for the absolute consequences that await them - when justice is being served. Compassion as the basic wish for the relief of suffering in all beings is connected to WHAT IS TRUE – and is the only way we are going to be able to begin to heal and move forward into a future that has a better understanding of the relationship between ourselves and the anger we are feeling.

We need to educate one another so that we can teach our children a healthy and productive way to move anger and the possibility of transforming it by understanding what it is in the first place. Taking responsibility is the first and giant step forward to a planet of peace. The only place we can work to eradicate this viral epidemic is ultimately within ourselves. To make that choice is critical because when we choose to blame one another and fight against each other, that is when we are most lost and feel so depressed.

I do not choose to sacrifice myself for the pleasure of another person's pain.

Additionally, I'll never again allow the false belief of viewing myself as being helpless and unworthy as I unconsciously once did. There is not a single thing anyone can do or say to change my past. I am the only one that can change it, simply by the way I choose to remember it and who I want to show up as today - because of it.

With this authentic reasoning, I have transformed the experiences of the past into the reality of my life of freedom today!

I am most grateful.

Made in the USA
San Bernardino, CA
16 December 2019